Due to changes in life situations, he has found his inner me, which has helped him write and have artwork shown at Koestler Arts. *My Ghost* was the best for him.

To my brother Curtis and my friend Chris Culley for putting up with me. To my Mum and Dad for forgiving my mistakes. To the rest of the family and most of all my children and grandchildren for enjoying my words.

Derek Harewood

MY GHOST

AUSTIN MACAULEY PUBLISHERS™

LONDON • CAMBRIDGE • NEW YORK • SHARJAH

Copyright © Derek Harewood 2024

The right of Derek Harewood to be identified as author of this work has been asserted by the author in accordance with sections 77 and 78 of the Copyright, Designs and Patents Act 1988.

All rights reserved. No part of this publication may be reproduced, stored in a retrieval system, or transmitted in any form or by any means, electronic, mechanical, photocopying, recording, or otherwise, without the prior permission of the publishers.

Any person who commits any unauthorised act in relation to this publication may be liable to criminal prosecution and civil claims for damages.

A CIP catalogue record for this title is available from the British Library.

ISBN 9781528960793 (Paperback)
ISBN 9781528964425 (Hardback)
ISBN 9781528965279 (ePub e-book)

www.austinmacauley.com

First Published 2024
Austin Macauley Publishers Ltd®
1 Canada Square
Canary Wharf
London
E14 5AA

Miss Georgina Gibson, my fiancé and PA. Mr Barry Gibson for his belief and trust. Alex Gibson whose poems helped me to see life. Mr Halon at Lewes Prison for pushing me to write. Ellie from Koestler Arts. Gemma from RIFTE for help to believe in myself. Mike and Helen Snell for designing my book cover and believing in my words.

Short Story

TO SEE WHAT YOU DON'T SEE.
I GOT TO SEE ME
OUTSIDE, LOOKING
IN.

My Ghost

Is this what life is? Thirteen years of schooling, nine-to-five jobs. Routines daily; hustling money, paying rent and taxes.

Blazing, getting high, usually ending up in a comatose state and feeling like you're up in the clouds... my God, what state!

Drinking horrible-tasting lager just to experience a wavy state, not remembering what you got up to or had done during it with uppers and downers for your mixed-up drug induced mind.

Is this what my life is? Those people who befriend you because of what you can get them on the cheap. Others relying on you because you shield them... Amazing! The life you enter, you come in naked, innocent to all. So how is it your life? Your ways are faulted by others who enter this life the same as you have done, yep, into this world! With no realisation of what, how and why? Or who they will be.

Different levels of emotions, anger, rage and even love hit whoever has been given the grace of living life, the life which affects all that are born—birds, insects, humans, even vegetation, an experience of some life's realities and troubles. All are different examples of nature's creations.

Is this life a lesson that never ends? Because in life, there is always a lesson that never explains why. WHY? We have curiosity of how we become and how or why our actions happen. The one thing in life that cannot and will not change is the emotional carnage that we, as people, entertain. It doesn't reason with good or bad in people. It doesn't let us understand the evilness and spitefulness that we, as people, in life have.

Also, life gives us more than one answer, more than one solution to the many problems we endure. Life has one element that nobody can beat. Life brings death, hence we people know ultimately death means never to come back. THE ONE DEFINITE RULE IS: We always say goodbye to loved ones. Yet, we have many beliefs of the unknown. This is what gives us afterlife experiences.

Think

Us as elements of life have the ways of routines of life; that is what we do, who we really are, why we live.

Scientists have their opinions and tests. Naturists have their opinions. Also, religions have participated with their own views. But nobody has the right answers to why I am here sitting away from life, stating these views and thoughts, or as to why and how life decides to place me where I am.

But nobody has the right answer. All have different outlooks, as I have told you we go through ups and downs, ins and outs of life's unpredictable routines and its rhythms; but in fairness, the answer may be that what is good for some people can be bad for others.

I mean in life, as we say, one man's waste is another man's treasure. Here I am writing things I think I now understand. Why me? Why my life? That always ends up with me having to understand 'why me' and people of similar ways like mine to be there for life's darker side to keep beating on us.

Not making my thoughts and actions revolt against life, but I now must step out of myself. Like a ghost staring at the outer soul of myself and my shell, trying to understand why. Why should my body and soul have to get my inner self to look at my outer? Not with pleasure, not with hate but with observation.

Observation of my outer self/soul, a ghost dealing with situations life has presented before me.

My inner is telling my ghost to SEE WHAT YOU DON'T SEE!

I am now getting my answer as to why I am here at this present time. I am here incarcerated by life's rules from judges and their peers.

Yet, even though my ghost is seeing where I am at, also the depths of my curiosity, my ghost is not accepting the outcome of my situations.

How could I be the one life wanted to punish? Why should I be the one my life would try to break? My ghost is looking at myself, still with no judgement of myself or pity. My ghost can see and feel my acceptance of my doings, but my ghost is wanting to know how and why. It is woken from my body. Why it is seeing me actually acknowledges its presence—me, myself, is not craving for freedom but craving to understand why life has allowed me to be in confinement. Why would my ghost leave it till now? For me to have understanding, the words of my father come to mind.

"YOU ALWAYS FOLLOW OTHERS. YOU ALWAYS HAVE TO BURN THE CANDLE AT BOTH ENDS. YET, THERE IS NO ONE TO IMPRESS. SO, YOU MUST BE TRYING TO IMPRESS YOURSELF. BOY, YOU CAN'T SEE WHAT YOU DON'T SEE, EH!"

Well, I am now here with my ghost outside of the inner me, watching the deepest part of myself come to light. As I am writing, my ghost shivers my spine. It won't speak to me, as I am not dead but my ghost is showing me I am not alone. I am to notice the inner me, which has now come to light. My ghost is showing me the inner me must be on the outer side of myself so I can realise the magic and natural possessions life has given me amongst all the heartache, pain, love's losses etc.

Within the emotional episodes my life has been through now, my ghost was trying to show me and open my eyes. I can cleanse my pains and my soul to believe in the magic if I believe in life. I NOW SEE THE BEST OF MY LIFE. MY QUEEN and MY FAMILY also see the worst of my life, not being able to accept my hurt.

I now respect my ghost for showing me that I let my common sense turn to stupidity by turning to drink, drugs and the blind and false feelings by letting myself be pulled into by the wrong associates. I must let in POSITIVITY. I am now being shown by seeing the normality of life. I do and will fit perfectly. I ALSO KNOW IF YOU CAN SEE THTROUGH MY EYES that you will see your own strengths.

I now know that I have no need for anxiety or depressive thoughts where you battle yourself. My ghost has taught me to know myself, a lesson well learnt. I tell you that for nothing amazing that being actually on the outside, looking in, being able to look at oneself to be your own judge and jury, that can be a dangerous place for one to be.

Remember your inner self is supposed to be wiser than your outer self, which is your shield and strength. You can be disillusioned if you do not take time to see and understand. For me, my outer self is my shield. Obviously, my inner is emotions and can affect all types of hurt and is where my moods come from. I no longer look at my life as a criminal but through the eyes of worth and value. As a person, you can be blinded, hurt by a past that keeps coming back in memories and dreams. YOUR thoughts become depressive and the anxious vibes creep into your mind, like a plague decreasing everything. Your thoughts become like a blanket smothering, taking your clean thoughts, turning them bad.

Suddenly, my ghost has a shiver go through me. My ghost is telling me to STOP. I am the blanket smothering myself. It is saying there is no need for this negativity. I realise my ghost is right and I must see the teachings from my life.

Amazingly, how being able to actually look back at one's self is wiser than the strength of your inner self because to be on the outside, looking in, can be soul-breaking and that can be a dangerous place if you cannot see.

Remember, your inner can strengthen your outer. Do not be disillusioned if you do not take time to SEE WHAT YOU DO NOT SEE and understand doing with the self. My ghost can understand where I am coming from. Then my ghost gives me a big kick, making me look around at where I am and what I am doing with myself.

To pass the timeless days go by, my life is now a story I am showing to face the lines on the pages of my experiences. Right now, I have a lot to go over about myself. My ghost is now my only true friend because my ghost is me. My ghost is now my best friend. It is by my side, involved in all my ways, now more good than bad.

My ghost is now showing me that life will always have answers for every type of living situations.

Life is life and can never be fully worked out. Life has two main scenarios—one birth and life—two deaths, and that is making me accept that even now, as a person, to help my way of life, I have fully understood what I can achieve. I now understand that I have abused life's disciplines and abused the fruits of nature through the drink and drugs. My ghost is showing me to come to terms with the way life has been and to come to terms with the changes that I need for myself in life. By showing me I am alive and that I am ready to face what is installed for me, I can now look for what is installed for me. I can now look at life with a different vision.

As I am preparing myself for change, my ghost is giving me the strength for change but before I change, I must understand and gain discipline for myself.

I do not want to lose my treasured memories but obviously understand that some must disappear. Losses and hurt must be replaced by adventures and persistency, so I do not fear change.

Understanding Your Ghost

I big myself up because I see myself. I see my ghost is there for me. I see my inner self is there. I'm now whole with that inspiration. Life, or the meaning of life, has put me in such a positive state of mind. I now can see what family and the people who care have been saying to me about my ways now I have opened to my ghost and my inner self. My sense and sensibility is so positive and strong. I am fully recharged.

I also see the bad and there is loads of it but I can now see that with a little good in your heart, you can defeat the dark side of life and now I don't have to battle myself. I now do not have to battle myself.

I NOW SEE WHAT I DID'NT SEE.

I did not see ME,

CRAZY IN IT.

Well, thanks for taking time to read these few lines. BLESS LATER.

Well, I suppose it all started in the mid-70s, young, coloured lad born into a kind, loving family, who had been starting a new life in a new country. The young lad had been living with two of his other siblings, two older brothers over the next few years. He got to know two more siblings—a sister and an older brother.

Well, this lad, I suppose you would say he had had an illness that wasn't understood till years later but, back in the day, it was classed simply as bad behaviour. Obviously, the young lad caused a lot of problems for his family but it was not intentional; he did not really understand what he was doing wrong (because he was acting by how his brain was telling him). This young lad was pretty quiet when out playing but he had a totally different onlook which did not come to light until years later.

He remembers his childhood. Unfortunately, it took being set up and a prison sentence to actually get to grips with life. Also, to think normally, you see in the previous years, the lad had grown to be well respected and well loved by most of the people in his life. The problem for him was he did not know how to love himself. His heart was strong. He always had an answer to help anyone, especially the ones life overlooked. Now he is on the last months of a prison sentence. That is where he actually found his worth. By that, I mean he actually found a part of him that was his, a part of himself that needed to be let out. Also, he now understood why he was starting to be called Bear (quiet but quick to growl and never backs down). He found that he could open to himself or anybody when his pen touched the paper; that was where he found my ghost. Or should I say his ghost found him. In prison, the lad, now a grown man, had to look at himself to try to understand how he was back in jail. Truthfully, there was no proper answer, probably if he hadn't told the prosecution to go f**k themselves and of him.

THE night was hot, had no air and a poxy 12x8 cell was shared by two men doing a 23-hour bang up. The lad, now a big man, was drug-taking veteran, but since he was back behind the door, he did not miss one part of that world. He didn't even have a comedown. His comedown was helped by his ghost but before we get to that, you will learn on how my ghost came from reminiscing.

Blue

Just gone, for New Year 2021, the celebrations going on at the time in the jail were whistles, doors banging and the officers on duty getting slagged off properly. At the cell door, there was a knock.

"Yo, Bear, you need anything?"

"Who's that?" Bear answered, knowing full well who it was at the door.

WHIZZ!

"Beg you, don't shout things like that out, man. Why do you have to advertise me like that? Last time I'm telling you!"

"No worries, uncs. I wasn't trying to get you knifed up. I was just showing some family love, no worries," was the reply.

The pen stopped writing. Like I said, the lad now was a big, grown man doing a prison sentence, but in this sentence, there was something magical to come out of it. He looked out of the window. He didn't really know why he looked out of the window. Maybe it was to escape the thoughts going through his head being that bit had just turned new year into a kind of depressive time the brain was on full depth of thoughts. Maybe it was because it was just a grey time for me, the only conclusion that could be thought.

Pen was on the paper, looking at the piece of work he had written about my ghost! What he did not realise was that my ghost was real; it wasn't just words on paper. True, my ghost was a part that everyone has in them, but they never really see their ghost because people find it hard to look at themselves in the real light of life. Only when we go through trials of life, those parts of the ghost appear to their hosts or themselves. A loud sigh comes out of his mouth as he starts to see the magic of the ghost unravel in his brain. Maybe I've done too much Class A in the past or maybe this is my way of coming down, or is this just what happens to your mind when you got nothing but time to yourself?

All could be thought. All could be said about my ghost but in all reality. My ghost did come to life in a way that you could not explain and a blessing it was to experience.

It was coming up to 10 o'clock, a Friday. The lads on the prison wing had got some luxuries and were in a quite tranquil mood. The lights were now going off in the background. You could hear the young inmates with their rapping spitting bars to one another.

It was going to be one of those nights where you wish you were at home or out with friends, one of those nights where you find yourself questioning how you got to where you are. The sorrow runs through your soul, yet you still must accept your surroundings regardless to whether you were guilty or not once behind the door life stops. You drift off to sleep in the end. Then for some reason, you awaken. Your body knows that you are in jail but your mind will not. Frustration overwhelms you. You breathe slowly, trying not to get on a downer, not to beat your sanity and then you stay awake, trying to work out what you have lost and where to start from once you are released.

In your mind, you try to reassure yourself of how things will be better when you are free. Then it happens; you start reasoning with your spirit. Your emotions start to come into play and your world turns hectic but what you have to realise is that that is when doubt comes into play. Also, it is when you start to fool yourself about the realities you have been through. You tell yourself lies to make yourself feel better but you know 12ft x 10ft cell is your world whether you were guilty or not.

It must be coming up to lights out. At around ten-ish, Bear was his usual sombre self. His mind was taken to another place as he thinks about my ghost—funny because it was like he was whole. He was complete. Bear reasoned with his thoughts when he heard:

"WHAT? WHY YOU DISSING ME?"

For a moment, he was in shock.

Did I really hear that? YEP, was the unexpected answer he got back. Bear sat down by his tele and looked around his cell. Why? He didn't have a clue. Now Bear was a person who didn't get scared so easily, so his frame of mind was just taken aback. For a moment, he tried to regroup himself.

Boy, you're going nuts!

Again, Bear heard a voice again. This time, it seemed as if it was mimicking him. Bear shook his head and looked at his Bible on the window ledge.

"Right, that's it," he whispers to himself. "I've done too much class, no joke. I'm frigging talking proper to myself surely. I'm dreaming 'coz you are hearing things that are not there."

"IS THAT WHAT YOU THINK?"

Bear froze. Taking a deep breath, he sat down and tried to hear the voice again; I have been through some crazy experiences in my life and I'm on one now, in jail. I really do not like this high. By that, he meant he had no answer for what he was going through.

For the next ten minutes or so, Bear waited. Admittedly, he was waiting for the voice to speak to him again but nothing. Bear then realised that something was going on.

"OH, YOU SUSSING IT NOW."

This time, the voice was loud and precise. "What the frig is going on, real talk, you some kind of ghost? If so, what the hell do you want with me?"

The answer Bear got back left him stuck to the spot; his face was now breaking sweat not through fear but pure surprise and shock.

"WELL, WHAT'S IT LIKE TALKING TO YOURSELF?" Then a chuckle came.

"This ain't funny now." Bear was beginning to wish he was drunk or high; this was the only way he could get to grips with what his head was doing to him.

"YOU CALLED ME THINK!"

"Ughhh, Parden, hang on. Why you in my head and why am I talking to you/me, whoever was the only thing?" Bear could say.

Again, the voice spoke. "WATCH, listen. SSSHHHHH. YOU HEARD THAT, EH? I AM YOU, YOU brought me out of you. THINK. THINK ABOUT WHAT YOU WRITE."

Bear was at a loss for words. His head was spinning but his aura was in sync with what was going on.

"Wait a minute. So I am not going mad. This is real." He pinched his leg to make sure he was not high or dreaming. "Show yourself." Then he said seriously, "This is nuts. I'm in Penn and proper, asking something to show itself. I'm going medical in the morning."

"YOU KNOW ME BECAUSE I AM YOU. YOU CALLED ME OUT through your work. Now think. You know me, for I am you now. THINK." This time, the voice was prominent and serious.

"Okay, give me time to regroup myself. I know you because you are me. Think about what I have written." Bear ponders frantically with his mind, then he sees what he was being asked. "Oh my God! Is this what I think it is? Sorry, are you who I think you are—MY GHOST? Is that you?"

Bear waits frustratingly for an answer. Time must be coming up to 2 a.m. The prison was quiet, just a sound of reggae playing on one of the lower landings.

Bear, his kettle on and tokes on his vape, waited passionately to hear the voice. Now he was intrigued and on an invisible high. *How can this be happening?* Bear waited but nothing but silence. That was what he got—silence. *How am I to sleep, eh? My days, God! What is going on? I have gone a bit scoody whiff, eh!* Finally, as the night turned to morning, Bear finally dropped off to sleep.

The morning came so quickly; it was as if Bear had just blinked and the doors were being opened for brekky. Bear got up, went on the landing to the showers, got freshened and then went to the canteen for his breakfast, which consisted of porridge, scrambled eggs and toast. He walked past the guards and other prisoners without even noticing if he was being talked to. Bear was called by the governor to come to the office. He had had some parcels to collect. On entering, the guv asked how he was and if he was feeling okay and why?

"Guv, don't. I look okay, uh. Don't forget, guv, we are in Penn. What is the right way to look?"

The governor answered Bear by saying, "I can't understand a fella like you, with your nature is in here."

Bear smiled and winked at the guv. "I'm here for rest. Street life was killing me, guv. Thought I'd pop in for time out. Is it okay if sign for my mail or whatever it is?" The guv nodded, handed Bear a pen and receipt for him to sign and then handed Bear a parcel which felt quite heavy. Bear went back to his cell. On reaching the door, he asked the guard on duty to lock him in.

On arriving through the door of his cell, Bear sat on his bunk and started to open his parcel, which consisted of awards letters from professional authors' books from them. He sat amazed. There must have been about seven copies of books, letters and appreciated comments and words of encouragement for him to keep drawing and writing. Bear sat up, taking notice of a letter from a well-known paper. When I mean well-known paper, asking Bear if he could sign for them to maybe show his work for future publications, wow! I'm on some kind of trip! This is nuts. I have to come to jail to achieve something, uh," he said to himself. "I am definitely out of my comfort zone." He sat, rubbing his head, thinking about what was in front of him. Admittedly, he was impressed because he was not really one for entering competitions. He saw a note from the art department, saying they hoped he didn't mind but they had entered his work in the Koestler awards and hoped this could help him get a career or help him when he was released.

Bear's spirit, for the first time in life, was high and this time naturally high. "OH, NOW YOU GOT SOME SPIRIT," it was the voice from last night. Bear chose not to respond to the voice. "DON'T IGNORE ME! YOU KNOW YOU CAN HEAR ME 'COZ I AM YOU."

"The voice said we have a lot to do; trust me. You have just had a taste of what life can be without drink and drugs but it is down to the belief and changing the whole persona of yourself."

Bear tried his hardest to not take any notice of what he was hearing but truthfully, he wasn't a fool. He was realising that it was him who, I suppose, called for help. He was also seeing that he knew he had to change everything he knew about himself, his outlook his street manner, even 90 percent of the people he knew because they were not friends, as they were only in his life for what he could do for them.

"Okay," he said, "I know who you are and I know you was damn rude to me last night, frigging ignorant, but then again it must be me. It must be me to understand what is going on." He took a few seconds to settle with what was going on.

"So whilst I am going through this nutty stage in my life, LISTEN WHERE ARE YOU." The voice was talking seriously, Bear was actually taking notice. Well, as much notice he could as well as looking at his awards but what kept flashing through his mind was that MY GHOST was something he wrote as a way to try and understand what he was going through as he sat in his cell. It was his way of not drinking and craving for drugs, which did not even happen; that was a touch.

"What's the time? Must be lunchtime soon!"

The afternoon went pretty quick. Bear phoned his family, (some) telling them about his awards. Then he went to the door of his cell. "Guv!" he shouted. The door opened. The eve shift was just starting to come on the landing.

"What's up?" the officer asked the Bear.

"I need to see Scouse. He wants me to draw some pics of his kid. Is that okay?"

"Go on. You got five minutes before we lock down. Cheers, guv." And Bear goes to Scouse's cell, knocking on the door. He entered.

"All right, lad," was the hello he got.

Scouse was a chirpy fella from near the Anfield ground. He was on the last of a 20 stretch, but on his landing, the cells were left open. It was as if you got to have a serious charge to have a status nuts in it.

"Yea, all good. Have you got those photo? Remember I said I would draw them? Got to hurry, guvs, at my cell door waiting."

Scouse hands BEAR six pictures, and he said, "Anyone will do. I'll pay you."

Bear replied, "No papes big man, out of friendship, check you morro."

With that, he went back to his cell.

"Cheers, guv, might do you a picture for a box of vapes if me door is left open sometimes." Then he winks at the officer and steps into his cell. He put the pictures in his drawer and turn on his tele time for the Chase. In the background, the noise in the jail was warming up new inmates coming on the landing poor sods, that meant someone was going to get terrorised. Why? Because in Penn, you have all types—shame, but it is what it is. If you cage animals, sooner or later, they bite also. In reality, there are bullies or people who have to show their comfortableness by putting up on hard-men acts over people they think are weak.

Anyway, I got my own problems, eh, thought Bear*, and soon I'm going to be out, so in reality, I got my own problems to worry about.*

Without that thought, he looked at his pen that seemed to be calling him. He stared at it and finally laughed.

"My mate, the pen," he said as he picked it up straight away. His mind was in thought about what he was going to write. Then he thought about what my ghost was trying to tell him—what is it I need to do?

*Oh yeah! Let go my past! H*e stared in thought, hoping that he would hear the voice of my ghost. This seemed crazy, me waiting for me to hear voices in my head, but if you break it down, it's just me finding myself. Have I really got a lot of luggage to get out of myself? I've been high for so long. I need to understand why I'm like this. That was the queue for a voice to be heard: WHY ARE YOU DOUBTING YOURSELF? OPEN YOUR MIND TO YOUR PAST. Then you will see where the cracks are that need fixing. Bear took a minute to think about what was being said in his head. His heart beat faster as he started seeing his life flash past him. He drifted back to when he was 12 at high school, his first. Back in the day, he ran with a crew of local lads from the estate, aged from 12 – 16, but truthfully, these young lads were tight. They were forever in trouble or on the run from the police.

These young lads were proper organised for kids. They never ran for any others but themselves. The lads also stood their ground from all corners. Bear remembered one time; the lads were going to the local school disco where lads from other estates turned. Bear remembered what he was wearing—black stay press trousers, black brogue shoes, a blue short-collard Ben Sherman shirt with a black box jacket. Now you think this was in the early 80s. All garments were brought from Lea Bridge Rd in London, also a trilby hat brought from Carnaby street. Also, these lads were part of the football scene they certainly held their own at home and away games. Anyhow, at the school function, it was nearing home time and the men putting on the function were tidying up. Bear remembered one bloke was sweeping up and had swept over his brogues. Obviously, Bear reacted with a bit of cheek, didn't recall what was actually said, but could almost feel what happened next. From behind, he shut off from the thought of his past.

"FACE IT," was what my ghost had to say. "It's just a memory."

Bear went back into his past, seeing the scene detail for detail, recalling hearing a loud bang and everyone staring at him. He then recalled his older brother asking him if he was okay. For a moment, Bear's mind went blank; all he could see was panic, kids running everywhere, but the one thing he did remember was that his crew was going crazy smashing the place and he also vaguely recalls a bloke holding half a broom. Then it all came back to him. What had actually happened was that the fella had swept up behind him, and because Bear had obviously said to his associate about sweeping crap over his feet, Bear had been smashed across the head with the said broom.

"Ah, I was only 12. Wow! See the world I grew up in my God. Bear took a toke on his vape as he saw himself being carried by his older brother and the rest of the crew laughing. He recalled the lads having to act like commandos all the way home due to the fact that the streets were covered with police on foot. In cars, it was manic. The lads knew every place to hide. It was a rush of adrenaline, truly a buzz.

Bear sat and thought, Couldn't even tell my parents…

That was his last thought about that memory. It was as if his mind didn't want to open anymore. Bear's pen twitched in between his fingers as if it were debating what else to put down on paper. He then got up and walked up and down in his cell. His mind was now on a roll. Thoughts were flowing through his head. My ghost was showing me something. Bear was now feeling free within himself because these past memories had been shut down in him, supressed for years.

Oh my God! he exclaims to himself. He had just had a thought about when he was in his teens and had been in town with Trina, a sad girl he was close with. On returning home, he had got a box from his old man right at the back of his head.

"Uh, what's that for!?" he shouted back at his old man, who calmly and sternly said:

"Why is your mother at the police station? What you done? You been stealing and fighting again." Bear recalled wanting to run out but stopped in his tracks.

"Mum's where? Why I haven't been with anyone except down Wimpey's with Trina? So why is Mum at station? 'Cause I ain't done nothing."

"We will see when she gets home. Now move from me."

Well, when his mother came home, she was in despair. At the same time, she told his old man that a certain friend of Bear's had been arrested and had said he was Bear, so when Bear's mother turned up to the police station and saw this person, he said, "Hi Mum, what's up? You know it's me."

Bear's mother chatted to his father about the incident and told him Bear had nothing do with any trouble.

"Boy, tell your friend them that they do not come down my path or even ask for you. You hear me?"

When bear had written the last word, he sat and thought,

That's what started me drinking proper. That was the same time my nan passed and then my grandad died the following year of a broken heart. He had been with Bear's nan since the start of the 20th century. *Wow! That is love in it.*

Bear sat in his cell with tears in his eyes as he remembered being told that he could see all the family sitting in the back room having dinner. He saw himself coming in and sitting with one of his brothers, who he was close to, but the atmosphere in the room was icy cold. His brother told him that his nan had died the previous night. Apparently, she had taken a fall and passed not long after the grandfather, however, had lost the will to live, rah! And died of a broken heart.

Bear, being Bear, stormed out of his house and got wasted, stoned, drunk, and that was where it started the road of forgetting and spite anger to the world. Yes, that's how he felt like life was a big lie; everything was wrong. There was no light, just hazy, foggy thoughts and a world that span round and round.

Bear put his pen down. He recalled he had only met his grandparents once when they had gone there for a summer holiday in 1972. It was best memory. He had tattooed on his mind that his grandfather was a no-nonsense man straight to the point about everything. His nan, however, called Mumma. If you understand the way I loved my nan, I used to send her drawings every month. He started to get agitated because he was getting emotional.

"DO NOT HIDE FROM YOUR THOUGHTS," my ghost said out of the blue. "You need to face yourself, your pains, if you want to see, see where your downfall is, so calm. Remember, it is me/you, our pain. I am your shield, so let me shield you." Bear stopped. "I got to get used to this whatever is going on then," my ghost said quietly in a whisper which actually tickled. "BEAR, remember why did the old man always say, 'SEE WHAT YOU DON'T SEE.'"

Time had gone quickly. It was coming up to lights out. The jail atmosphere was calm, no real noises or situations, bet the screws are in their heyday. Bear laughed. He picked up his pad and got onto his bunk. His mind was quite tranquil for the way he had been facing his past; it was not a really bad one but it was a wasted time of his life due to his drug habit which was the next thing he wanted to try and think about but there was one problem with that. Bear did not really believe he had a drug problem in the past.

"WHY LIE TO YOUSELF? JUST OPEN UP AND THINK."

"Give me a break," Bear told his ghost. "I don't even know what is happening right now. I know I'm Penn and I know I got to start my life over basically, and I now know that I have a third-person vibe going on. What I do not know is am I thinking normal or is it because I'm on some kind of a relapse again?" he laughed and let out a big sigh. The atmosphere in the cell was weird. Bear did not know what to think.

"This can't be normal can it? How is it that there is only you in the room, yet the atmosphere can be so rank all from thoughts or your own aura gets a downward vibe?"

Bear makes a note of how he was thinking and his thoughts. He knew he had to accept the way he thought and the way he looked at everything; the reason for this was that he was seeing the real him, the him that forgot how to live and how to enjoy. Time was getting on; now he was getting ready to get his head down, wondering what his sleep was going to be like and what was he going to have running round his Barnet (head). In reality, he was a bit uneasy; if his past came into his dreams, it would be hectic trust.

With heavy eyes, he sat back staring at the walls, as usual with music playing in the background on his radio. Looking at his pad, he tossed his pen onto the side and put his pad under him. He lay on his back. He looked into the night, seeing the different tones of darkness and shades of navy and distant lights from the stars. He thought, *What I would give right now to be there!* With that, he closed his eyes.

Into deep sleep, probably the best sleep he'd had since being banged up, his ghost was right; facing one's past was a way to get a good way to relax. But he did not realise that he was going to have a rollercoaster of a week mentally. Nothing comes easy, especially change.

The door opened for breakfast and he showered. Then there would be two hours of association, then locked up till the next day gym if your number comes up, BEAR wearily sat up in his bunk. The door of his cell was left wide open by the officer. Guv Bear called out, scratching his head as he got out the bunk. "Guv!" A head popped round his door. A ginger-haired officer smiled and casually asked his problem.

"Yes, Guv, because you leave my door opened so wide, just lock my door back. Sorry, no can do get up; come on breakfast then association or else a nicking."

"Oh, one of them days, is it?" Guv you grown bollocks that were turning adults now.

"Have you? Shut my door!" Bear shouted at the officer and kicked his door. The officer laughed and walked off, shouting back, "One more bit of crap from that gob and you will get a nicking."

Dickhead bear shouted back. He then grabbed his shower stuff and headed to the showers after freshening up.

He went to the top landing to see Scouse and the other lifers there, on the top landing. You didn't feel like you were in jail. He turned his head to the landing as he saw the screws legging it up the stairs. There seemed to be a nicking going on. The end cell was opened and three screws run in the cell, bad mistake. They flew out quicker than they went in. Bear called Scouse and gave him a wave of the hand. Scouse nodded his head and whoever was in his cell slipped out and back to their cells. At the end of the hall, more officers were coming up the stairs.

Bear wondered who was in the cell. It did use to be occupied by Manny. Manny was a Manchester hood massive but 'coz Bear hadn't seen him for a while, he just assumed he had been moved on to another nick but he was wrong. Manny came to the cell door covered in blood and a makeshift in his hand. In his Manchester accent, he threatened the officers and warned them that someone was getting striped.

Bear had time for Manny even if he was nuts to Bear. He couldn't believe Manny was a hardened killer with at least eight to his list and on his last of 25 straight years, but with this situation going on, he wasn't going to be going home for time.

"Is that our MANNY?" Scouse asked, someone better go calm him down, look their banging us back up. The stare he gave Bear was a look of help him.

"You know he listens to you." Bear looked back at Scouse. "You owe me. Trust ." He strolled over to the end cell. "Keep back, go back to your cell." An officer approached Bear. Bear looked straight at him and replied Guv,

"Back off. Manny ain't going to listen to you and you know someone will get hurt! Move. BEAR. TELL THEM TO BACK OFF CALL MEDICAL I NEED MY meds. Bear calls out to Manny, big man we good yeah? look. I'm going to come in. Tell me what's going on? You got five minutes. Then he is going to the block," says the guv on duty. "And explain to Manny he is straight to the block or the whole landing will be locked down."

Bear nodded and muttered under his breath, "Dickhead," as he entered Mannie's cell. He was shocked. There was blood everywhere.

"My God, what the hell?"

"Bruv, what's happened? What you done, Bruv?" Bear stares confused at Manny who was covered in slashes. Blood was dripping everywhere.

"Had enough. I'm done. What am I to do when I get out there, ain't nothing there for me family gone. I don't know how to be free. I'm done with it all."

Bear shoves his mate's shoulder and simply says, "Why don't you council? You know crooks, you know death, you know how to get young ones' attention, rebuild by working in the same topics that got you here, no better teacher than someone who has seen the other side. Think about that. Look, I'll get your meds sorted. You know you got to go block. I'll get you everything you need sorted but calm my G with them, screws don't care about no one, if they did that would be a first. Stay calm my G and I'll have a word with the Guv come blood."

Bear walked towards him. Manny looked up. His eyes were like he was on speed wide open. "I'm good," he said without a change of expression.

On hearing that, Bear tapped his friend on the shoulder and told him to go block quietly and to hold it down. Bear left the cell, saying to the Guv to allow his friend and that he had run out of his meds, so while Manny was in the block, the doctors and shrinks came to check him out. Bear then looked towards his cell where he saw a not-so-happy officer still standing by his door. He nodded and shouted, "Soon come, Guv," and took the slowest walk back to his gates.

The officer slammed the door behind him, saying as he walked off, "One Day!" He muttered to himself.

"Yeah, yeah!" Bear shouted out with a smile. He sat and took a vape out its box and had a couple of tokes on the plastic fag and sat back on his bunk. The tele had been put on for background music. Bear slipped into a morning daze.

"Wow!" Bear woke up. Jumping up, he looked about, shrugging his shoulders, looking around his surroundings.

"Life is nuts. You never know what cards you are dealt with." His pen was back in his hand. He rolled it between his fingers as his mind tried to work out, all that he was going through. He smiled to himself.

Have I actually got my life back? He wrote on his pad, PAST describing at time from his past, he pondered on whether he should write or not. Bear's mind was overcome with memories and past events. Hours passed, or that's how it felt. Memory after memory flashed past, his thoughts in the background of all this. Bear could feel his ghost wanting to verse an opinion but Bear was too engrossed in what his mind was doing, with mixed up vibes and drifts of emotion flowing through his soul.

Why is it? When you wanna think, you seem to suffocate yourself.

Memories came flushing through Bear's whole body, a truly emotional experience. People can tell you of dreams and thoughts BUT nobody really shows their internal feelings or thoughts.

For a brief moment, Bear was well lost in his thoughts as he came down or out of his thoughts. He was now able to be getting ready to write; words flew fluently from his pen. As the words appeared on his page, Bear felt strength from his words. It was hard to explain how free and relaxed he was. He started describing the area that was the centre of his tale to the right. There was woodland area around the park/field. Towards the main road at the south end was a railway bridge and a mini roundabout. Four or five youths were loafing around, smoking weed and having some beers which they had stolen from the local shop. While they were chatting, a fella—drunk, really drunk—staggered past the youths. Not looking at the lads, he calmly tried to control his steadiness as crossed the mini roundabout. He then climbed a fence and clambers up the embankment towards the railway tracks .The lads watched in awe, each of them noticing him at different times, each of them thinking the same thing: *HE AIN'T, IS HE?* The smallest of the youths pointed but never said a word. Today was a day to haunt two of the lads.

They watched as the fella looked back them. They heard the train, and it was like time froze; everything went in slow motion in awe. True enough, the old boy turned back to see the oncoming train. Then in an instance, he was gone. Life seemed to really, really slow down as the youths looked in disbelief. Bear paused writing as he thought about the confusion and actions of the incident. All he could do was sigh. *Why?* Well, the way he was feeling down about was by what he had written. He was one of those lads who saw this event. He realised now he had to change his outlook in life. Bear started to feel a bit down, thinking about his outlook. His spirit was feeling lost, not a good thought, eh? But as he sat in cell, the only thing he could think about was the lads in his story. What was going through their heads, and did they feel like he did?

The cell door opened for dinner, back to the routine of bang-up. Bear went down to get his dinner. On his way, he checked with the Guv about Manny. Bear then chatted to Whizz to get him some bits and pieces.

"Don't forget drawing materials, okay?" Bear finished chatting and grabbed his lunch and ventured back to his cell. On his return to cell, Bear had a few officers come to his cell door. He stood up, ready to kick off, thinking he was getting a nicking. To his amazement, he was given more awards. Now without realising life was showing Bear that it was changing, and boy, was it good! Bear was soon to be released and that was another chance for him to try and live free and contented. Soon he would be able to express himself in words, on paper, something he was now starting to enjoy. Also seeing how much a certain lady had shown him how to change and not buy words either, he was on his last few weeks. He wasn't even going to be allowed to his house and that was due to prison licensing. He had to be basically exiled if you can understand that. Hell! He even put that on paper. This was what he wrote:

I was in the pub off my nut on cocaine. A pretty lady walks up to me and expresses how good-looking I was.

He smiled proudly at what he'd written, the reason being that 20 years later, this same special lady was in love with him and he with her, even though life was the way it was. There would be more to come, the magic you get once in your life trust.

I don't quite understand. Life has many chapters for me, Bear thought to himself, *but what if I and the said lady break up by rowing, that's what couples do—row. That would do my head in. My God!* Bear thought to himself. What a lucky man he was, had now really opened his mind and could now understand what life was really about or so he thought; it had slipped Bear's mind that he was in a point in his life where he was going to start all over again, REALLY.

He shook his head in disbelief, so much going on in his head but Bear knew if all these changes were going on. He then had to really change as well. Bear had a sleepless night. His mind kept on thinking about the dark times that happened in his life. He then heard: *GOT TO HANDLE THESE EMOTIONS. REMEMBER IT'S US SORTING OURSELVES OUT.*

Bear listened to see if his GHOST had anything else to say or was it that Bear wanted to be shown how not to be affected!

Morning came. Bear was so tired from having a horrible night. He was in one dark frame of mind. He went to his cell door and called for the guard. When the cell door was, open Bear said to the officer, "Guv, can I go to meds? Having bad time sleeping and you know I used to drink snort and smoke pipe. I think my comedown is kicking in, as you know I'm a med case."

The officer looked at Bear. "Med case, you are just nuts. Go on; make sure they write down you didn't put app in (application form to see medical)." Bear was totally stressed out, cursing, listening to his ghost.

Why? Have this dream? He thought to himself as he walked to medical on entering. He gave his prison number to the medics. He then asked the medic to put on the records that they saw Bear without an app being sent in and asked for pregabalin. That was what was on script. When he was out on the street, he went back to his wing and made his way up to his cell, hollering a few bods on the way. Bear then popped into whizz's cell to grab what art stuff he could. In this sombre mood, Bear knew that his only get-away from jail was his writings and his drawings, especially the ones he drew for the other prisoners. He had taken two tablets, making sure he put them away (pre-habs were as precious as cocaine in jail) but Bear was a changed person. He knew his limits were on point and he was clean, his system pure for the first time in his life.

All Bear wanted to do was get on with what had been writing the previous night and he wanted to get out on paper why he was in this dark mood his memories were troubling and he could feel a shadow falling on him. He went through his artwork and found receipts for his work that had been entered in to the art competition and read some of the messages he had received from some of these famous authors. There were two that stood out for him, a book *The Artist Way* and a story in cartoon form where the author had put himself in the cartoon. I think his first name was Darren.

He forced a smile. You see when you are from the addicted life, you find it hard to take in realties, obviously 'coz your mind is in a haze. You might think you are in control but you are not. Bear shook himself as if to throw off this way of thinking. He knew exactly where the two authors were coming from in their books. Right now, he needed to get into his own story. His ghost was right; to be free, you have to face your past in order to be free in your new choice of life. Some things are hard to face but it has to be done. Bear would not wish for anyone to abuse themselves for as long as he had done to himself over the years. With that in mind, he put his artwork down and picks up his note pad debating to write down the memory that had come into his dream. The more he thought about this memory, the more irate he was becoming. This was new to Bear, as he used to be someone who didn't really to worry, but now he had become aware of how he had actually abused himself without realising. He also was trying to control himself, like his ghost said to get on with changes, you yourself must change too and that means that the first step to do that is honesty and not blag or excuse any wrong you have done in your life.

Standing in his cell huffing and puffing in awe of his thoughts, Bear's mind delved into a period he was out of control on drink and drugs. It went back to around 1996. He was living with two of his siblings, playing Dad during this period. Bear was steamed up every day. He had nothing better to do, as he had come another town where he had left because of heartbreak and also learnt that there is no real friends or so he had been made to think.

Bear could remember that day as if it were yesterday. He was in dispute with his baby mother and had just opened his front door and was starting to walk down the garden path when one of his brothers turned up winds down his car window and with a serious expression, said, "MUM's got cancer; deal with it," and drove off. Bear walked to his house which was 10 minutes from his siblings. As he got through, he found a letter with news of his oldest sibling who Bear had never seen but always been in touch with. With some dark news, she had passed away due to a kidney failure. At that moment, Bear came out of thought and was back in the world of prison. He shivered and stood up and looked out his window, looking for the tree that he watched wither in the winter, then flowered in the spring but it wasn't there.

Feeling down in the dumps, he recalled how he dealt with all of what he learnt. He called his friend Li'l MAN, WHO MOVED ON THE STREETS WITH HIM AND WAS ALSO HIS COd. Bear then fixed up his mood as he remembered him and Li'l M had got into his Rover and drove. Whilst driving, Bear remembered telling Lil M that they were going to see where the road take them; that was another story trust.

At that precise moment, Bear stopped thinking about his past. His Ghost so happened to appear to him.

HOW YOU DOING? HARD, ISN'T IT? FACING MEMORIES BUT DON'T STOP; YOU ARE NEARLY FREE.

Easy for you to say that, thought Bear. Then he growled at himself for talking to himself. *That's what nutters do.*

WHO SAID YOU WEREN'T NUTS? was the answer from his ghost and a little chuckle went through Bear's head, which he tried to ignore.

This memory made him want to get high. He looked at the pre-habs and thought he'll just snort three of them and I'll be buzzing, then he felt like he was being pushed and heard an angry voice in his head.

IS THAT WHAT IT TAKES? IT IS AN EXCUSE WHAT YOU ARE THINKING OF DOING, RUN AWAY DREAD, IS THAT WHAT YOU ARE?

Bear understood his ghost was right. He had fallen back into his old frame of mind but was being shown how he dealt with personal situations in his life that he had no control on.

Bear was now trying to control his way of thinking. He knew deep down that his ghost was right. It was down to him to control his thoughts; he knew right from wrong and maybe he was in the right place to do this in prison, so he did not have to drink or do drugs. He then looked properly to what he had achieved for himself. He was starting to see and learn where his weakness was, and to think in all these years of his bad habit, he could have sorted himself out but he only knew how to help others but not himself. Now he was learning to help himself. He had passed the first step in changing his life.

Bear put away his achievements and put his kettle. He then sat down to toke on his vape and thought how he dealt with the situations he had been thinking about and realised that he did try and run from the hurt. His daughter had passed, his mother was sick and all he could do was drive till he came to a beach where he and his friend sat with a crate of champagne and as much amphetamines as possible.

What a dick! he thought to himself, but at the time, he really did not know how to deal with the news he had received, but life got him back for that; it surely did. The lads, Bear recalled the way he had been off key, they got high, so high life meant nothing. Being high was everything. Now Bear realised that in those days, he did run to drink and drugs, so the bad sides of life he did not have to face. Unfortunately, it was by choice.

Those that do their addictions by choice are more dangerous than those that need a hit. They look at drug-taking in a different way and therefore never admit to being hooked.

True that. Bear agreed with his thoughts. *We used upsets as a doorway to get high. Now I have to use the positive actions and achievements to keep the respect in myself to keep away from that world. Walk in the park.* Bear tried to reassure his soul by saying 'walk in the park'. *Time yet again was now getting on if I carry on like this. I'll be out in no time.* He chuckled to himself. He was now getting to grips with himself.

That night, he had another memory hit him. It hurt so bad. He had tears in his eyes. It was a memory that nobody or any parent in this world should go through, and also it was the real reason Bear's drink and drug abuse went to its limits and carried on for another 15 years.

Wow, I have really abused myself. Lucky, I am not dead.

YEP, YOU'RE DAMN RIGHT, was what he heard in his head. His ghost was having an angry snarl at him. Bear tried to not think about the situations that were now smothering his brain but he had opened the doorway so here went 15 years. Prior to him being in Penn, he got a phone call from one of his offspring telling that he had to get to the hospital on asking why he was told his younger daughter was in labour, so he casually responded, saying, "Well, get Mum to go. I'll finish work and come down."

"No, Pops, you got to get here now."

BEAR, on hearing the tone of the voice on the phone, decided to borrow some money off his mate whose nickname was Shorts. On getting to the hospital, he made his way to the maternity wing where he saw his ex-partner, his three daughters and some other siblings from another relationship. Bear never even questioned who he had seen or why they were there. He made his way to his daughter's bedside where she cuddled him and pressed the buzzer for the nurse on entering the room. Bear recalled his daughter saying, "My pops is here. Can I see my baby?" Well, this is where he got the shock of his life.

The nurse walked in with a box or more like a shoebox. Bear looked over her shoulder, expecting to see some form of crib. His daughter called him to look. BEAR stopped his thoughts for a moment to wipe his tears. His ghost said some reassuring comments to him and then finished by saying, FACE IT. IT IS YOUR PAST. YOU HAVE TO LET THAT FEELING GO!

Bear listened to his soul and went back to his thoughts, taking a deep breath. He recalled what he had to see. It was a beautiful body of a baby at first. Then the reality hit; the little bub was gone up in heaven, if you understand what he meant. Tears filled Bear's eyes but look, he was a dad, so he could not show his pain at what he had just seen. This was when life stopped for real. It was like the worst high you could ever go on, yet at the same time, he had to carry fatherhood in a different way that he would not wish on his worst enemy. His ghost intervened his trail of thought.

You must accept the incident, yes, you got shocked, yes, you felt lost but think how your daughter was feeling and her brothers and sisters, also the nan, you have to let go the hurt and understand what they asked of you had to be done.

Bear went back into his thought. This time, he was toking heavily on his vape. He grabbed three pre-habs was just about to drop them when guilt hit him.

Look, he thinks to himself, *look at how you are running from your thoughts. Face them. Put those tablets down now. Face your past.* Bear put the tablets down as he recalled what he was seeing, bless young blood, had just getting his eye lashes. Also, Bear could see his skin was in the process of covering the veins and vessels fair play to his daughter who was now in control of herself.

"Daddy," she asked, "could you draw him for me so I can tattoo him on my back that way he lives?" With a tear-stained face, Bear recalled not agreeing, so he took a picture of little man and put his phone back into his pocket .When it was time to go, he kissed his kids bye, spoke to his ex-partner, then got the back to his gates where he cracked up emotionally as he drew the image on his phone on his art pad. Bear jumped out of his daydream as he heard the cell door open. It was the nightshift checking he was in his cell.

BET YOU WAS GLAD FOR THAT? It was from his ghost, actually sounding sincere in Bear's head, but he had to he was Bear innit.

Bear sat calmly with his head in his hands.

That's all you can do in here is think, think about this, think about that but what I should really be thinking about is what the hell am I to when I get out? No home, time on licence seeing probation officers rah! all that even before I'm free.

"Rah," Bear said to himself. *Another day is over. These thoughts are for real.*

Jail can rape you mentally because, like My Ghost says, all you have is time. He makes a final cup of tea for the night, his mind blanking the odour of the prison and blanking the noise of tele and radios playing in various cells. As he sat alone thinking of nothing but home, his head in turmoil, a whisper he heard. He listened and thought was that I or his ghost, it was what he thoughted I; it was his ghost, showing Bear a well-needed insight of himself.

My ghost was a lifer saver for Bear, who said to himself, *Soon it was going to be time to face normal life. I have to seriously evaluate 'my life, I know, that there is no choice but to have these changes. Maybe God has a plan for me. Prison has been a walk in the park for me and now I have my artwork and literature are now going places, now it's down to me.*

Bear realised that since he had been moved to this last prison, he was not being affected by the 23-hour bang-up. By being able to pick up a pen and paper, he had come down off of drugs and booze he picked up his pen again and started to write:

How can this be? Am I really behind the door?

This is real, missing my kids, missing my life, my freedom, my dog—bless him—has been put down by the police but yet there is no reports of the dog ever hurting anyone, up for repossession for a debt I never even caused, yet I am in jail doing better with my art and writing and yet I'm still nowhere in life. How the hell can this be? Bear was having a proper one on one with his ghost.

His ghost said, *NOW YOU ARE SEEING WHAT YOU DIDN'T SEE.*

It hurts when your eyes see the small print, Bear answered.

His ghost wrote like there is no tomorrow. *I keep drawing like a madman, I don't miss getting high, nor do I miss the drunk side of my life.* Bear realises there is a fear factor that he had overlooked.

BEAR WAS NOW UNDERSTANDING how much life was going to change for him, even though he felt broken. He now realised with the help of his ghost, he was actually fixed. He saw that he had now really lost everything but his ghost had shown him that God had a perfect path mapped out in front of him. His ghost told BEAR THAT HE HAD DONE WELL IN THE TIME. HE HAD BEEN IN THE PRISON SYSTEM, AND THE REALITY WAS THAT BEAR WAS NOT USED TO BEING NOTICED BUT NOW APPRECIATE BEING PART OF THE RIGHT SIDE OF LIFE.

The actual reality was that while Bear was in his cell, his drawings and writings were being entered to loads of competitions but there was one piece of work that had caught every one's eyes and attention. It was a story in a story and if he got into it and took it real seriously, may be it could change his life for real. It came him one night and that is how his ghost WAS COMING TO LIFE, SO THERE WILL BE MORE. As life change, so must we.

ALL well and good, Bear was on the last of his prison sentence and he was ready to change his foolish life on the out; mind you, Bear still did not have nowhere to live. He was going to give one of his daughters' address so that he would be let out of jail and have to wear a tag bracelet on his ankle. At the same time, he hadn't even planned what he was going to do to survive on road. "Argghh!" he let out that frustrated sound, then did the usual cuppa and a vape. He then turned to his cell door and gave it a kick as if he were being kept for nothing. *Wow!* he thought. *Right. I wish my ghost was about.* Feeling his thoughts were about to get stressed he laughed. *I am going mad.*

With that in mind, he went to stand by his door and waited for the cell door to open for showers and breakfast.

Bear acknowledged some of the inmates as he was due to be drawing pictures for them, also it was well needed, these little deals.

Maybe my ghost will show his opinion could really do with his insights but how come if I am, he and we are the same how come I am in need of his advice?

'CAUSE YOU DO, came a little chuckle as deep voiced as it could. *CHAT LATER,* was the next response. Bear nodded his head in acceptance. After Bear had freshened up and had brekkie, he decided to go and put his name down for the gym.

Most of the morning was quite chilled, no real dramas or incidents. It was as if the prison routine was normal life, normal outside life. Bear's mind was so stuck on going home, changing life for himself that he didn't even realise that the governor was talking to him and actually giving Bear more certificates. Bear came out of his thoughts.

"Sorry, Guv. Didn't see you. They were miles away. Now I'm back. What time's gym?"

"Not too sure, got a lot of staff off with Covid, so you have to tell the lads to bear with us. Yeah, no worry, Guv. Are they for me?" he asked, pointing at the certs in the guv's hand.

"Soon be out, won't you? Don't want to see you back look at your achievements."

"Well, Guv, you never know, eh! Get back to your cell. Someone will be round to let you know about the gym, okay."

Bear bowled back to his cell and sat looking at the amount of books, certificates, drawings and letters from professional authors and artists. He felt so proud of himself. He was now really understanding his ghost. He was actually seeing where he was going when he left the prison.

He could now see a meaning for him being off drink off drugs. Bear was seeing what he did not see for real. It took a rude awakening from life to put him on the right track. Now Bear had to do what his ghost was telling him.

You have to be real with life, honest with your good and bad sides and face all realities, NOT use your past to run from, 'cause most of us don't run. We hide in drink and poison of the drug world but if you come from the other side, you must understand that everybody has a ghost and you just got to face the ups and downs in life and not get misled, that's a fact. Every person has down days but when we cover them up with booze or drugs, don't be fooled. Yes, you might go round thinking you are in control but that's is an out 'n out lie to one's self-trust. Listen to your ghost. It is just you showing you there is time for anxiety, depression, loneliness, heartache and pain. It is not to run from; it is to stay and evaluate what one is going through. That is where you learn to listen your ghost. Your ghost is the first voice you hear, yours! Bear had to really sit and take time out to understand his life.

Rah, this is where life is going to be different, he thought.
STOP THAT! THERE IS NOTHING TO BE UNCOMFORTABLE ABOUT.

Why is it when people go through things, they always make a task of situations?

You back then doubting me, why? Bear, I am you and you are me, but have I now been over things with you. No one said change is easy. Remember, it was you that brought me out of you. His ghost continued to badger Bear's thoughts. *All I am trying to do is honour and help you but do not forget; I can only be here for you if you are there for yourself. Belief is hard if you have not had anything to believe in, you have to open your eyes, mind and heart and open to your past.* His ghost was trying hard to make Bear understand what he has achieved by being off drink and drugs, to open eyes to see what he had actually done whilst been in prison his stretch had been long soul searching period mentally draining but refreshing due to the achievements he had done for himself.

OPEN your mind now. You are clean. You are still not free from distress but can now be strong to deal with it.

Bear listened, shaking his head with agreements and disagreements that he was hearing but for the first time in his life. He could see what life had in store for his future. He also knew that he still had a few more dark nights in Penn to get through before his release that meant more emotions had to come out him.

Bear looked at his clock, seeing it was now coming up to dinnertime. "Today's gone quick. It's like nighttime can't wait to come," he mumbled under his breath. He sat and had a timeout. He got his pencil and started to sketch a picture of a little boy's photo he was given the other day. This drawing had a meaning. You see, the lad who had given Bear the picture had never seen his kid, reason being no visitors because of Covid. Also, he had split with the baby mother the day after he was sentenced (gutted lad got a dear JOHN). Bear started to draw the picture.

That had to break you losing your girl the day after getting locked up, bless, this picture was going to be one of his best drawings. Bear smiled at the kiddies' face in the picture and said the lad was going to break some hearts. His mind started to think about his own kids. "Got to give them proper time when I'm out," he muttered to himself, "when I get a new place mind."

The cell door opened. "Dinner," said the officer with a smug look on his face.

"So what, Guv, no gym, eh?"

"Sorry, but we haven't got enough staff. This Covid has hit three of the orison wings, so 23-hour lock up."

Bear cursed under his breath and went to get his dinner. On getting back to his cell, he stared at his masterpiece. He was quite chuffed. Drawing seemed to come when he was going through any emotions, chuffed because drawing seemed to naturally come for him, but he had to be emotional.

Man was going to be chuffed when he sees this. Bear sat and blazed on his vape. Then he turned his tele on just in time to see the news. As he watched the state of the world during this pandemic, Bear realised that he was actually better off in jail as the whole world was on lockdown. *Crazy in it,* he thought admittedly. He was glad because now people can understand being owned and told what to do is not nice; it is soul destroying. Bear then thought about how he was giving his opinion to the tele and concluded, *I am definitely not getting banged up again. Look at me; this is not me anymore.*

Bear felt pride racing through him. He was now transfixed on his experience with himself, teaming up with his soul/spirit. Not many people even come close to meet their inner self. This is an experience that should be taught to help people. Bear thought long and hard. He was now seeing what he needed to do when left the prison. True, he had to definitely stay away from his old life, but truth be told, Bear knew that he could never actually leave the streets behind just the wrong uns no more time for wasters. He took a long toke on his vape as he blew the smoke out. He tried to ask his ghost a question, half-heartedly though, because he had that foolish am-I-talking-to-myself-again vibe. Bear laughed at himself.

I should know better. Man has to learn how to handle his own company. I don't mind my own space, so how come in Penn you let it affect yourself? His eyes went on towards the picture he was drawing as he looked at the little lad's innocent expression on his face. A warmth flew through Bear each time he looked at the little un's face. Bear could feel that what he had drawn was actually something that could stop people from breaking. Imagine the kiddies' pops had never seen his son and also got *Dear John*. The day he got sentenced, Bear realised the strength he was giving this bloke just by making him feel better through a drawing.

Then Bear got a response from his ghost.

OH, YOU NOW SEEING WHAT YOU DON'T SEE. Now can you understand the words of your old man used to say? You/we, I have always felt like we are on the outside the different one's but the truth is that you/me are not no different to anybody else; in fact we are more in tune with life because I/you look from the outside in and try to evaluate whatever we are going through but what we are learning now is that drink drug abuse was there as a saviour in a way that it did save you, Bear. It saved us inner and outer. We are now complete because we are now thinking about life. How it should be? It's just a shame. It took one hell of a party life to have such a sad ending to now have to look back. Bear all of a sudden stopped thinking and looked at the kids' picture again, realising that it took a drawing from someone's sorrow to see life rah. *Is this how it is?*

Bear was beginning to see how much he wanted the life that his elders used to tell him to get. He could now see that to be loyal. *To be free, you must accept yourself and your mistakes without no prejudice or regrets because we cannot blame anybody for our actions except our own selves.* Bear now had to actually think that his mind was now going to go on a rollercoaster of a ride. *Some would say he was anxious, not Bear, who would never agree to anxiety because the system is making a profit of an invisible illness which is not really an illness; it is simply people overthinking about things, overthinking, then panicking but the system is not helping people. You cannot argue with yourself but when you have no one there or here, WHAT DO YOU DO? Trust, think. Everyone wants a perfect life but if bad things happen on the news, then why can't it happen to you? THINK. You do not see you have to believe that your decision is right. Belief is the greatest thing for people, anyone, but remember what you believe in you must back it. There is no place in life for falseness or lies. Especially if you are telling it to yourself.* Bear downed his pen and looked over what had been written. He had a smug smile on his face. He looked out of his cell window, thinking, *Rah, I will be out soon but what am I supposed to do considering the way life has gone for me also coming out of* myself? *Truth be told, my God has shown me how to understand life and also taught me to see myself through my ghost because my ghost is me and truthfully, the best lesson came from being somebody to nobody I shit you not, I have grown in sense but by being taught by realities of life, so I must pass this lesson on.*

Finding My Ghost was probably the best thing that has happened to me for real. Look, I'm in Penn and I'm having to find MY WAY.

And I now pen to papers is the way for me, so God bless and watch over you, me, whosoever because as I have learnt there is always a story, if not mine, then yours—BLESS.

This is from Bear and there is more to come. I have experienced life sweet but harsh, so if I can help you change, keep reading what I write because if you are reading, then you are the same as me looking for a place to fit in TRUST AND KEEP READING MY WORDS because everybody is a somebody, okay!

Bear looked at it, his last words, chuckling to himself,

Should have been a comedian, a lot easier than writing, mind you, they must write their acts down so ain't no different.

Bear sat looking at his words, trying to understand how he was truly seeing life in a different light. Also, he was now understanding that by living in the world of drink and drugs, he had abused himself and lowered his own standard of respect. His ghost was right; the way to get on was to see the past and face it. That way, you become free when you realise that you have lived in the shadows, the way to get to the light is to face and see your rights and wrongs. You cannot changed life without strength and belief which does take time.

Bear looked around his cell, feeling suffocated by his mixed thoughts. He was hoping his ghost would link with him but he could knew you can't always get help when you cry for help! Rah! Bear was now out of dream world. He toked on his vapes and looked at his drawing pad and the last pictures. Then he told himself, *That's where I want to be in a picture.* He then laughed and wondered what the next few nights were going to be about. He knew his comedown was mental and not physical.

Time was not even existing at this present moment. In a way, it was a blessing, but it was also turmoil.

When are they going to open and let us out? Bear thought. *Did you know that when behind the door, you mentally suffocate yourself.* Bear banged his cell door. When it opened, Bear told the officer to give medical an application for him.

"You okay?" asked the guard. "You don't seem yourself."

"I'm good," replied Bear, knowing he was in cluck could be his only explanation. The door shut. Bear heard the officer open in 10 for gym. "Okay."

His ghost came to him and reminded Bear that he needed to go through this and reminded Bear the way he was feeling was because reality was now being dealt with him and by him a new path. *I'm lost I'll be out soon but to what?*

Bear sat on his bunk, trying to control his thoughts. He knew that over oncoming nights, he would have to face himself and his past but knowing that he had to face himself.

I suppose people would say he was anxious to him. It was another high a natural one. Bear grabbed his pen off of his table and his pad. Looking over his writing, his memories were flowing back in himself. He was searching for the dark times that he had blocked out. He turned to his window and stared out of his cell window, looking. He looks at the clouds. He smiled because he used to tell his little ones if they were not happy or if they ever wanted him to look into the clouds and let the thoughts float to the clouds. This was how he had to deal with his demons.

When you are in the world of upsets, you shield yourself to escape from the pains and emotions. Sometimes, we search for the right answers and get the wrong answers. Then we get high and drunk. Basically, we think that we are forever fighting a battle, so it's easier to blank it out.

Bear's adrenalin level was racing a situation; he had left blocked from his mind floated back into his head. At the same time, his ghost appeared to him and assured him that he needed to see this memory to help himself. Bear trembled. Nobody tells you of the bad sides of intoxication or drink or of the lowness and self-pity episodes. You have to face, and being in jail wasn't the ideal place for someone who was in the drug and drink trap. YOU ARE THINKING THE WRONG WAY; that type of disbelief is what kept you in that world and your frame of mind.

Right now, your comedown is put on edge because it is unseen and your spirit is coping with it totally differently, hence you calling for me through pages. The pen was your comedown mechanism, BUT you cannot get over your pains and accept the ways of truth, truth to yourself reaching out for help from the outside. His hand was twitching as he started writing words on paper. Within minutes, his thoughts were out of his control, memories flashed by not in order but all the same, his eyes swelled with tears.

How did I blank this rah? His writing was now flowing as he remembered getting into the SUV, acknowledging the person who was driving, smiling at her for a long time. Bear recalled then his thoughts went toward to being in a hotel. On entering, he opened a can of beer which was in left pocket—nice room, good staff. Bear didn't see there was something troubling the lass, who seemed to on edge. Bear's heart was now racing. His brain fast-forwarded. He seemed himself sitting in the armchair and his friend crouched. A tear ran down his cheeks as he thought of that day. Bear, whilst talking and swigging his beer, recalled seeing a dark shadow appear from where his friend was sitting. He shuddered as he pictured this memory. He could feel himself wanting gear but he shut that thought down and stopped writing for a moment to regroup his thoughts. His ghost showed him a way to deal with his uneasiness. *IT IS PAST. LET IT OUT. Deal with it. Understand why this happened.* Bear toked on his vape, tapping his pen on the pad and away he went. This time, he was in the zone like a fly on the wall.

Kinda spins you out if you can see your thought or memory in detail, especially when you realise blood was the shadow on the bed. Bear recalled asking how come she was on her period. He didn't know what to say really. The pen carried on, moving and writing. Bear took out a bottle of Bacardi which he had in his bag. Taking a big swig from the bottle, he looked at his friend who was trembling and trying to cover her sad, embarrassed look on her face. A sigh came from Bear. His pen stopped for a second. Bear listened to see if he could hear if the officers were doing the gym run. He then got back to his thoughts. His mind flashed here and there for some time. Then *bang!* Pen back to pad, he felt a cold sweat at the back of his neck.

CALM! I FELT THAT DAY. I CARRIED YOU THROUGH THAT EPISODE. THAT WAS A NERVE-RACKING EXPERIENCE.

The look on the poor friend's face was heart-breaking. His ghost was helping Bear remember the severity of the incident. The only problem for Bear was that it was someone special to him from his past and he wasn't ready for what he was about to be told.

As he saw the panic on her face, he kept wigging on his bottle as if it was going to help make this better. Without thinking, he stripped the covers and carried his friend to the shower where she curled up in the corner. All she kept saying was, "I'm so sorry."

"Sorry for what? You have nothing to be sorry, for nature is nature." Bear was trying to ease her embarrassment. He was three-fourth the way through the bottle which obviously had Bear merry, then recalled asking his friend if there was anyone he called. Bear, a bit intoxicated, then tried to scrub the blood off the bedding with water and salt. He sat with his back against the bedroom wall. Guzzling the last of the bottle now, he was in control of himself. *Knock, knock.* It was the food that had been ordered, which he took quickly and shut the door. He then gave his friend a couple of towels and taking them, she said 'thank you' to Bear and proceeded to explain how she got in touch with him and why she wanted to be on her own. Bear listened and tried to tell her she didn't have to justify being sick. Then came the slap.

"I wanted to see you because I wanted to let you know that I am not well." Bear sat up looking around for his bag where he had more booze and a ticket (cocaine) which he nervously tackled whilst being told his friend was dying from cancer in the stomach.

The pen dropped on to the pad. Tears came into Bear's eyes. He looked out of his cell window and cursed under his breath. His ghost explained to him that he should not blame himself through someone's sorry but understand that his friend must have really loved/cared for him to be able to want him to know her situation.

Bear calmed himself, picked his pen up and carried on. The friend was in a dressing gown and looked so frail. Bear told her not to worry about the bedding and come sit down calmly. And he chatted with her for some time when her phone rand, going off his nut at her. You could by the defensive answers she was giving. Once the phone was down, Bear was asked to leave, as her family was coming to get her. A taxi was called and they gave each other a hug and Bear left on entering the taxi. Bear broke down partly. He was so drunk and also he saw cancer. He called one of his brothers and told him of the dramas he had just been through. The taxi dropped him off at his mother's.

Bear told his parents what events had just unfolded and he grabbed his mother, telling her how sorry and embarrassed he was for not being home for her when she was diagnosed with the big C within ten minutes, was back in a cab, going to his daughter's, where his bags were also his knives and other artillery. The kids were in bed, so he crashed on the settee where he commenced to partake in hoovering (snorting and drinking) as his eyes closed. He drifted into a light sleep. He then heard his daughter calling him. As his eyes opened, he could see the luminous colours of high viz in the distant hallway. He rose, saying to the daughter it was okay, as he got to the door. Bless his little grandkids, who were up, staring at him and the figures in the doorway. "How are you?" Bear asked her without thinking. That's when he had to actually wake up. It wasn't ambulance; it was armed police. He stared around his cell. His mind snapped back to reality.

The pen stopped writing. The day had gone so quickly; it would soon be dinner and then banged up till the next day. Bear was deep in his emotions, trying to understand what he had written and also justify because this lady he was writing about, he had not seen her for 40 years. She was his first love and now to see and hear the way things were for her in her life.

Bear looked at his pad engulfed with emotion 'coz he just could not believe how he handled the situation. He continued to pick up from where he had stopped. He smiled when he wrote. Bear looked at his daughter, telling her everything was okay and to get the little ones back to bed. He then casually said to the officer to wait. He was going to use the toilet and dashed in to it. Whilst in the loo, Bear proceeded to snort whatever was in his pocket. He then rinsed his face and went back to the front door to be handcuffed and get put into police car.

"The cell door opened dinner," the officer said. Bear put his work on his bunk and proceeded to the lunch queue, agreeing to grab some photos for his drawings. He then grabbed his lunch and hurried back to his cell. On arriving in to his cell, his door goes Uncs. "Can I get your food?" I'll sort you when we get canteen."

"Yes, take it, whizz and get out my gates. I'm writing bruv," was Bear's answer.

Once the cell door was closed, Bear carried on writing. It felt good to get this pain on paper and to see how he had treated or rather how had abused himself by running to drink and drugs. He got back to his story. It was so relieving to get his pain out of himself. His ghost was right; facing the past had to be done.

Well, I might as well get right into this, banged up till 'moro anyway.

Bear thinks deeply about being arrested and being told that the said lady had been found facedown on the hotel bed with blood coming from her private area. I recall she was constantly saying, "Forget the charges."

How is she? Bear thought, but that was my reaction because I couldn't believe what I was hearing. Bear could see the smug looks from the police that had arrested him—smug bastards!

He saw the time in the cell and then the release. The said lady had undergone emergency operations throughout the time of his remand in the cell. Then he recalled his release without even an apology. It turned out when his friend had come to her senses, the police had told her that they got the man who had assaulted her and she didn't have to be scared. They had egg on their faces when she told the exactly what Bear had said word for word.

Bear's memory ended on this note. He had not seen her since the police had erased all information from his phone and hers—why? Hell knows, mind you, she did find a way to get hold of him about two years after the said incident to let him know she had always loved him and felt sorry for the way he found out about her illness.

The pen went down. Bear stared out of his cell window, thinking how he could do with getting high and drunk, but he knew that was how the old Bear did things slowly, he started to smile because he now could understand about letting your bad past go.

If not for his ghost coming out of him, his hatred for his life would keep him from a decent and blessed future. Bear relaxed on his bunk, pen down, memories fading, letting him be at peace with himself. He now could see how much of life he had wasted by running to drugs and drink; that was the easy way out but now actually seeing himself and seeing his worth by the awards, he had got also being noticed for his artwork.

"Thank you, God," he said out loud. Why? Because Bear had even sold a drawing from work that had been entered into art exhibition at the KOESTLER ARTS.

With all this running through his mind, he dozed off with contentment and pride. "My Ghost," he hears himself saying, "NOW YOU UNDERSTAND IF YOU WANT CHANGES, THEN YOU MUST CHANGE AS WELL. Remember, there is more to let go before you are free in yourself."

The next morning, Bear was up before the door opened for breakfast. He was thinking about what he had written the previous day and how more settled he was feeling. He had to admit his ghost was making him observe himself. For this, he was thankful, but Bear knew he had more pain in his cupboard to face.

The day went by quickly. Bear went to the gym. Then after dinner, he sat in his cell drawing and reading. When it came to lock up, Bear picked up his pen and started to think about the times where he ran to drink and drugs.

"Wow!" he exclaimed. "I run to that crap and made any excuse to get it or rather get high."

Funny facing yourself is harder than facing an enemy. Reality is. There is no right or wrong way or no excuse for the way he had punished himself with those poisons. His cell door opened. It was association that meant two hours of mingling with the lads on his wing.

Bear stood in his doorway, watching a few weasels running about getting their spice. People were swapping their meds. *What the hell am I doing in here?* Reality was hitting

Bear, as he was on his last couple of weeks before his release. This day felt different to him; it was as if he was in a foreign country. Lost, he sighed, went back in his cell and slammed his door. "Where's my pen?" he said under his breath.

What was our worst moment besides what you have already written? He asked himself what he was going to put on his pad. Bear stopped and looked at what he had already written. He was stuck. He sat on his bunk thinking about his children, wondering what they must thinking about his present situation.

The pen rolled about in his fingers. Bear was starting to realise that not all things could be put down on paper. Some had to be dealt with accepting DEATH, comes to his mind. Dark thoughts swarmed into his mind. His heart started pumping. Some might say he was feeling anxious or panicky. He flushed back to a funeral he had been to that broke his heart. "You probably know how he dealt with that."

Bear mumbled this to himself. He imagined how he would have been if this didn't happen. At that moment's thought, his pen raced to the paper. It was as if the pen wanted him to write about his pain. I mean the pen was writing words faster than Bear could think. Not long after the incident with the lady friend who was sick, Bear recalled a period. He was on self-destruction that was when he lost his god-sister. They were so close; the pen trembled in between his fingers. Then back to the pad, Bear was in a dark place. Yet again, the feeling or the lust to get high was smothering him. He could taste the beer his soul was begging for.

ARE YOU FOR REAL? FIX UP YOURSELF. WHAT WOULD YOU TELL YOUR KIDS IF THEY WERE GOING THROUGH SITUATION? his ghost piped up.

"Thank you," Bear said to himself; that advice was what was needed. Bear collected himself, realising if anything, he was dissing his god-sister by including thought and the lust of drink and drugs, basically the want to get high that was a wrong thing he had done at that time when she had lost her life. It was an excuse to get high. Bear looked at what he had put down. He could now see through clean eyes the way to honour her was to stay on the oath he had found in Penn and to clean himself up and to follow the journey God had given him. Bear knew that he had to make his god-sister proud of the path he was to be on.

Bear appreciated his ghost intervening and also allowing him to see his past self. Bear stopped writing the way he was feeling; he didn't think that he could face anymore of his past. He knew that life had really changed. He was now understanding properly what his father meant by saying, "SEE WHAT YOU DON'T SEE." How could he be so blind? Bear saw everyone else but not himself. Rah! It took a false imprisonment to wake him up.

Surely, 40 years is a long time for the self-medicating, Bear thought. *Look at what I have been through. Frigging imagine first time in Penn I was in detention centre.*

Thirty years ago, then Bedford, then 20 years ago, Woodhill. Most of that was in solitary confinement, now to date Lewes to Rochester to Peterborough. Now look at me, soon to be out with more than I came in with and that isn't no joke, now got to start all over again.

NOW YOU CAN SEE THE RIGHT WAY! Bear tried to ignore the voice in his head, but he knew that obviously his ghost was him. Well, his soul, if you understand his situation. Bear stopped by, moving his pen on the windowsill, looking at his phone. He went over to it and started to phone members of his family.

That was his first step. He let his children know where he was. Then he phoned his parents, apologising for letting them down and he also let them know he told the prosecuting solicitor and the jury to go f**k themselves. "It is what it is," he said to his old man. Bear then added that he was better off in Nick; it gave him rest and time out.

His father asked if he was getting smashed on the spice. Bear reassured his pops that he was clean and he was on point. At the end of the day, Pops said life had changed without no warning, so he must change.

Bear's pops was a man of very few words. Bear was totally in debt with him. Bear then apologised for being a menace when he was younger and thanked his father for being there for him in the past when he was in bad way. Bear said his goodbye to his parents.

Sitting on his bunk, staring at his pile of drawings, then turning to his pile of books and finally his certificates he had accumulated. Sighing, he cursed under his breath. "WHY did I have to be here? It is what it is." His mind wandered around his cell, laughing to himself. It'd be the last time he will have to see those green walls and that was for sure; even though he had spoken to family, Bear was more at peace with the fact that he was now understanding himself and accepting all his faults without making it some else's fault. To be truthful, Bear knew he couldn't blame the drink and drugs for blinding his life but he was now woken up to the fact that he let himself get controlled by the feeling, the high, and when he was low, he let himself chase the get-high feeling. Bear scratched his head. He realised that his subconscious had helped him to come out himself to see himself. Bear knew he was lucky and accepting if he had not been dried out by being incarcerated in the system, he probably would have killed himself by indulging too much.

In the background, he heard a scuffle going on the landing. Bear listened to see if it was someone he knew. All he could hear was Smithy egging on the commotion. Bear collected up his belongings and put them neatly under his bunk. Ignoring the scuffle, his hand was itching to write, so out came the pad.

Once turned to a blank page, the pen was on it in a flash. Just finishing work, Bear wrote. Three other lads were working with Bear. For builder Ernie Jackson, they had come into the residential estate not far from a nursery school Ernie pulls the van onto the path and parked the van. There was a commotion, so they walked to see if they could help thy made their way through the crows of screaming kids. There were teachers who had faces like ghosts. Bear looked at his boss and then started to shout at the numb teachers. Whilst Ernie tried to on coming parents to his dismay, Bear saw a little boy on the floor. He went over to the young lad who was, or seemed to be, gurgling.

Bear's head started to spin. He cleared the onlooking kids who were not crying truthfully. Bear knew in his heart this young lad was on his way to God; his head was squashed. At that point, Bear pulled his pen off the pad. It was tripping him out that he was writing this event down. He shuddered and returned his pen back to the pad the pen and trembled as he did. He stopped and made a cup of tea before returning to writing.

Before he put pen to paper, Bear got his tea and poured a circle on the floor in respect for all the people. He had known that was what he would if he had a beer in respect for the honest and angelic who had passed.

With his mind on all who had passed away, his pen carried the boy was still alive but obviously it was too late to help and the sad point was his poor mother must be on her way to get him from school. With that in mind, Bear remembered putting his index finger in the little boy's trembling hand, which gripped Bear's fingers. Bear threw his pen on the floor and put his head into his hands as he visually saw the incident in his head but he was glad he let it out of him. Bear remembered that he went on the most drink and drug session that lasted maybe 10 to 16 weeks of his life.

Breaking from inside to out of his mind, Bear couldn't even remember what he indulged with. But now he could see he was hurting for little and his mother and that poor kid held, well gripped, his finger. Bear was never going to let that thought go; he would keep that was a memory to keep forever in respect for the boy holding his finger him, gripping his finger, Bear thought.

Boy, I recall I got proper messed, never again, he heard his ghost. *ANYONE CAN SAY THAT BUT IT'S UP TO US TO MAKE SURE!*

I know! Bear responds. *Time to respect myself and whosoever I care for.* There is no reply. *What you gonna do if I don't listen to you then?* Bear thought in his head. No answer. Did he get back silent for two or three minutes.

Then My Ghost calmly replied, *I AM YOU. YOU ARE ME AND THAT ONLY MEANS YOU DON'T LISTEN. I GOT NOTHING TO SAY. SO YOU OBVIOUSY WANT TO GO*

BACK IN YOURSELF. FIX UP, MAN. THIS IS WHEN YOU NEED YOUTHE MOST. THAT IS WHEN YOU GET REALEASED.

Bear felt foolish. It took a few minutes for him to understand what he was saying as he calmed himself. Bear realised that he was only dissing himself. His ghost was his common sense. Obviously he was to change, and he was in the process of rehabilitating by understanding that he now saw himself first and foremost.

Being straight and sober, he realised just by being in jail for a small time. He could see how life has everything for every situation. He was getting deep into his thoughts for a couple minutes as he came out of trip. Bear shook his head, laughed at the way he was thinking and he muttered, "See jail? Huh. See what it can do to your mind, especially if you're not guilty." He laughed and put the kettle on as he had a sudden craving for tea.

Bear looked around his cell, thinking that never again would he let the system do this to him.

All because getting high or smashed, now I'm in proper reality, now game on. Bear looked at the kettle, watching it boil. Then he switched it off.

All over again must he rebuild his life. Truth was that he hadn't a choice at his age. His ghost muttered in his head, *Nuts innit.* Bear agreed with his ghost. He then lay on his bunk and let his thoughts fly round his head as he drifted off to sleep.

Bear was in a deep sleep. His dreams were heavy. By that, I mean he was being taken back to a phone call he received whilst in the first part of his sentence. The image he was seeing was as if he was there. Tears were streaming down his face as he slept.

The phone call he had got had broken him. Deeper he was being tugged into the nightmare, to the point that he had to battle himself to wake up. He sat up wiping his eyes on his quilt, jumping out of bed. He started to write frantically.

LOLL was a close person to Bear's family. (She was his god-sister; his father was her godfather.) Bear recalled that she was just like Bear, a self-medicator, but he had always kept his eyes on her but this time, it was too late for him to be there for her. "God bless her," Bear called out as he wrote. His ghost awakened and whispered to Bear.

THIS THOUGHT HAS TO BE LET ALONE ONCE YOU HAVE OUTED IT ON PAPER. YOU MUST LET IT BE!

For a moment, Bear was cursing and tears were coming out of him like a waterfall. He carried on writing but the words he was filling the pages with were out of pure and utter rage. He describes how she was found and the positioning of her body in every detail he has been told.

Bear looked up from what he had been doing, stared out of the window at the night sky, sweating. His hands were sweaty, his mind empty. Truly, this was one incident. Bear had to release also the pain and vengeances he had in his heart.

YOU MUST LET IT GO. UNFORTUNATELY, LIFE HAS ITS DARKSIDE but YOU MUST TURN YOUR DARKNESS INTO LIGHT.

His ghost was taking over his moods and actions; that was the best thing to happen for Bear, who was now looking at the pages he had written and let out a sullen sigh, adjusting his thoughts, letting his ghost control his mind and thoughts.

I am getting out soon. It is not wise for me to get out with this pain in me, look at my positivity and talents I have to understand this pain as the same as understanding that my whole life has to be revaluated, must let this pain go and not react on it, rah life, my frigging life.

LIFE IS WHAT YOU MAKE IT AND YOU MUST ALLOW AND UNDERSTAND THE WAYS OF LIFE.

Bear shook his head, trying to make sense of what his ghost was saying, knowing full well his mind was trying to show him the right but, in his heart, Bear knew that he could never stop hurting over the murder of this person my li'l sis. Bear used to call her but once he was on road (free). She, not being about, was going to be a hard one to deal with. It seemed like the nearer it seemed to be getting released, Bear felt more and more pressured. He could only explain the way he was feeling at a point of not knowing, being in the lurch—why? Well, when your life has no answers, you either panic or ignore the oncoming situation, sometimes better to not know is the easiest way to deal with oncoming traffic. He surmised to himself. The high was in the not knowing. Bear could hear his name being mentioned on the landing. He strained his ears to listen but couldn't hear the conversation. He could pick out one voice. It sounded like the officer in education and the day-shift governor. The cell door opened, and he was asked to step out of his cell.

Bear sat at the table on the landing. He was joined by the pair of officers who seemed unsure in what they were doing.

"Problem?" Bear asked with a smirk.

"No problem. We are not sure of your release terms. Can you give us an address you would be staying at and the postcode? As we understand you cannot go back to your dwellings for the terms of your licence."

"Wait a minute; you mean I can't go home unfortunately?"

"No."

BEAR stood and went back into his cell, slamming his door behind him, muttering a few swear words at the officers.

They knew he must stop with family and knew it would be three years before he could go near his crib. *Why waste his time mentally and physically stressing his head, eh?!* A pink form is posted under his door. Bear stared at it and then put the form on his desk, muttering.

His ghost was obviously feeling low from Bear's thoughts. Bear looked at his pen and pad and his ghost was on form TRUTHFULLY; Bear listened to his thoughts.

HEAR ME. WE GO THROUGH UPS AND DOWNS AND INS AND OUTS, BUT IN REALLITY, WE STILL HAVE TO SOLDIER ON. His ghost was trying to keep Bear in a positive frame of mind. DO NOT FORGET THAT YOU STILL HAVE A FEW MORE EXPERIENCES TO LET GO BEFORE LIFE CAN MOVE ON. That was a reminder from his ghost. Bear looked out the cell window staring into the sky looking, searching for that little bit energy to pick his spirit up.

Why? Am I searching? Why am I on a low? Maybe because reality is now round the corner or maybe it is because I am still in this cage. Either way, life has got me on a downs. Bear looked around his cell. His ghost tried to relax his spirit by making Bear think to himself how different life is when you are not under the influence of drugs and alcohol. Bear was appreciative of this vibe.

Bear picked up his notepad and his pen whilst debating on what to write. The pen rolled between his fingers. Then words rolled from the tip of the pen onto the notepad. He started by writing:

At this point in my life, my ignorance and obviously by living life through intoxications the path I have walked, I have no regrets.

My ghost has shown me that the way forward is to accept and try to understand my own participation in how my life has gone. My ghost has helped me to understand my life and its outcomes, in a way that I feel blessed to that I can finally move on. Life has many paths. There is no right way truthfully to have the perfect life; by that, I mean there must be millions of terminologies for that one statement alone—PERFECT LIFE.

My ghost has made me understand that every person in life has a story some good, some bad, some emotional, some even so terrible and unbelievable. But all the same, every one that lives, there is always a tale.

There is no time limit in how we achieve targets. Limits are different for all types of goals and for all types of people, but what a lot of us who spend time in our lives are feeling like we are different or like there is something wrong with us, that is so not the right way to be but like my ghost has shown me. In the world I live in and through some of my own experiences, I have overlooked the fact that life is to be lived, mistakes are supposed to be taken in and understood not to be used in a blame game. There are enough paths for everyone.

My ghost has also shown me that as we have all types of good and all types of bad; everyone has a place to fit in good or bad, trust! Every day brings joy and pain but you can't live life without any positivity. Some people have dreams, some of us have ambitions, some of us have good work ethics and others do not.

Remember your past and remember your dreams for your future but as my ghost tells me and shows me there is a thin line between judgements and thoughts in this world of ours, but there is magic, love, beauty, even harmony in this world. There is a place or situation for all walks of life. Which is yours?

Everyone has a ghost or spirit/soul but we always second-guess ourselves. Also, self-doubt can destroy our outlooks.

The one thing I have learnt is by acknowledging my bad points have made me see the good in myself. Also the good in life. Life's choices can be harrowing and scary but that is where teachings and being able to advise and help others by learning through what we experience. Well, I think I know what I mean.

Bear took his pen from his pad, placing it on his desk. He sat and listened to the activities going on his prison landing. He had drifted from the situation.

SEE IT. DON'T MEAN YOU CAN'T GET FREE. FREEDOM IS A STATE OF MIND IN YOUR CASE. His ghost picked up Bear's spirit yet again. The pen returned to the paper, writing instead,

Of darkness in my life, what or where are the good, warm moments?

Bear wrote without even thinking.

I see and know that there has been some good times and some magical moment but it will be some time before my mind and soul get that warmth back, the reason being is that I indulged with the poison (drugs and booze) and you do lose the detailing of events and you drain not just your caring; you drain your positivity and beliefs, hence becoming lost then you go back to your safety net drink and drugs. Why? Because know how to live but thinking like that is a cop out.

His ghost showed Bear that until the day he passes from this Earth, Bear will always have a chance and always have a story.

THAT'S WHY YOU GOT BLESSED WITH GRANDKIDS. Your tales will help them.

RAAAH. Lit out, Bear could hear the night staff coming on duty touch today.

Went fast. I'm tired for once. He put his pad and pen down and relaxed on his bunk. He had a weird vibe like something was in the air but what he couldn't say.

His ghost whispered into Bear's mind:

LISTEN. REMEMBER THESE WORDS. TIMES OF CHOICE, WHY? BECAUSE AT THE MOMENT, YOU HAVE A FEW WEEKS BEFORE YOU ARE FREE, SO YOU MUST TAKE THAT TIME TO HELP YOUSELF ADJUST. Be ready for the next chapter of your life.

A time to be born and a time to die
A time to plant and a time to uproot
At time to hurt and a time to heal
A time to tear down and a time to build
A time to weep and a time to laugh
A time to mourn and a time to dance
A time to scatter stones and a time to gather them
A time to embrace and a time to refrain
A time to search and a time to give up
A time to keep and a time to throw away
A time to break and a time to mend
A time to love and a time to hate
A TIME FOR WAR AND A TIME TO MAKE PEACE.

The Change

Bear was now released, but to do what? You were away from reality in Penn, and there was an uncanny feeling in the air, as well as a high from simply being on the outside. One thing was certain: My Ghost was going to be busy. OBVIOUSLY, HE WAS PART OF BEAR. When Bear left the prison gates, he was lost. He walked for a while, then returned to the prison only to see two of his offspring looking at him seriously. But he knew that he was still on licence for three years, nuts in nit, but what people do not realise is that now Bear's sentence is now beginning.

He was obviously on the road, but because he was on a licence, he was in limbo; in his mind, he was all alone, but he couldn't show his pain or upset. He had his children and his family, but that is when you have to be strong with so many people upset because of your sentence.

"Raaah!" he exclaims under his breath. "This is b***s at my age, I must start all over again, but I have been placed in a town that I despise; I lived here 20 years ago, and now I'm back." He slumps by a café, looking at his bags. A smile comes to his face, and he feels a warmth. The bags are filled with his awards and pictures, as well as nearly 40 books sent from producers, authors, and artists. Bear now has a sense of worth running through his body as he stares at his new world.

Suddenly, a welcoming voice enters his head: "ALL REAL NOW!" My Ghost is back in his head. "Look, I think you were once a proper mash head. Now you have a chance to change your life. You are alive, and now you are what you have told many people: that you are free to do what you want. Well, now's your time to prove it."

The Change of a Dream

My Ghost was the magic of nature for Bear as he passed one of his offspring, he asked for a pen; that was what he needed. He asked his daughter if he could use her yard as a c/o address so he could write; his hand was itching to get on paper; as he sat, he got his pad out and the pen couldn't wait to write.

'My Ghost entered my life at a time when I was lost.' The pen rolls between Bear's fingers. Bear sits comfortably and looks out of the lounge window. Then he stares at the clouds. His mind remembers when ever in the past his young ones were upset, he would tell them to look at the clouds and let whatever was upsetting them go and be blown into the sky. Bear's pen hits the pad. His main topic is understanding what My Ghost had actually done for him, so off the pen goes. My Ghost was showing positivity, not judgement, to Bear and how he had self-medicated in the past, also being on the wrong path. My Ghost also made Bear's inner come out. The pen lifts off the pad, then it is back, and words just seem to appear on the page. 'Life cannot be taken for granted. Most people have experienced bad times, emotional turmoil, and times of being nowhere. By nowhere, I mean loneliness, which is one of life's motions.

'My Ghost has shown that when the average person has good, warm times, they forget the strength and glow because, when the bad times hit, people of different attitudes, temperaments, and levels of emotion can be disillusioned and perceive their situations differently.

'Therefore, My Ghost was showing Bear the meaning of his existence in his life! The one thing that was shown was

Bear having to face his upsets, accept how life has ended up, and learn from the movements of his past.

'The thought of rebuilding is daunting, but by understanding that everyone has a ghost, some good, some bad, or so we think your ghost is you, so if you see life in one way then Bitt shall be that.'

Bear stops writing and looks around thoughtfully, thinking that *yesterday I was in Penn, feeling no value, and now I have achieved a lot by being truthful to myself. Now I have to believe in myself and not be swayed by my past or the uncertainty of my future,* Bear's thoughts of self-doubt are interrupted by My Ghost.

"Self-made confusion," he tells Bear that the unknown of the road ahead can only be dealt with by keeping your dark thoughts away from your light thoughts. Life has many ups and downs ahead no matter who you are, young or old. Bear puts his pen down. His mind flashes back to the prison; he felt more secure there. "Raaah, look at how I'm thinking—what the hell is wrong with me?"

"Nothing," replies My Ghost! You have now to believe in your path; you know you have changed, and you know you feel like you can get your dream, but you must find it in yourself to gain strength from positive actions.

That night, Bear stayed at his daughter's and tried to plan his new life; he actually stays at her place for a few weeks, mainly drawing and putting pen to paper. One day, his daughter calls to tell him that he has some official mail. Feeling a bit panicky, he gets his mail. There are letters of all sizes. "You know what these are." My Ghost pops up and says, "Look at the name on the letters to see who they are from."

Bear looks and has a warm glow flow through him as he opens the letters. He notices that they are certificates and pictures from an exhibition, as well as letters from a person who actually bought one of his drawings. Bear has been given the boost he needs to feel like he is worth something.

"See," My Ghost says to Bear, "we have the opening now and it is up to you to realise that there is a future, but it has to be worked on." Bear knew that the way he thought now as a straight person, he had to take time to think and also be strong in his thoughts as he would sometimes drift into his dream state of mind that has to be controlled.

But seeing how much he had achieved from prison made him quite overwhelmed. My Ghost shows BEARS he has to embrace his achievement but he also has to realise the amount of work it will take to rebuild. First, he had to get on the road and make his life back in his way. Bear needed to feel whole again, and that was not going to be easy. What was emotionally draining was that being on the outside of people's love and caring can be a weight on you because you naturally feel like you must keep proving that you are ok.

My Ghost tries to show Bear that it is the way he observes, "LISTEN I am you, and you are me as we have been each other, so why do you persist in stressing out? Once you had to let go of your bad memories, but have you not understood that now you must bring out the good memories to give you your strength back and drift into the warmth of those past events?" It takes Bear five minutes for his mind to go back in time. The energy you use to remember is nuts.

Leys Hall was a place that stood out in Bear's mind. He recalls going to dances back in the day with his parents and other siblings. He feels the atmosphere and imagines the elders drinking rum and playing dominoes in the background to the sounds of calypso music. Bear feels the warmth of the memory. He sees his mother dancing together with his father, which was magical. He then sees himself and his brothers playing pool with his cousins.

The vibe he got made another thought enter his head. He chuckles as he sees his father organising day-trips every August bank holiday; there would be the old man's crew picking up family and friends. Bear puts his pen down and looks at the part where he had two or three coaches taking everyone to the seaside. There were always the elders to the front and the youngers to the back of the coaches. Reggae music would be playing, and the atmosphere was magical. Fried chicken, curry goat, rice, mangoes, and fruit sweets. Bear stops thinking and wipes a small tear from his eyes. How had he forgotten those trips?

Bear was being emotional, but in a happy way, as his mind went on another trip. Scotland was what he thinks about, laughing to himself as the memory became clearer; going to the launderette to do his washing, he recalls leaving his wife and two young men and saying they would be back soon.

Bear decides to pop on the bus whilst the washing is in the machine to have a game of pool. Well, that was a bad move. Bear has a few games of pool and a few spliffs, then, like a mug, he decides to drop some acid. Well, he sees a coach, and because he was in space-head mode, he gets on it, totally forgetting his washing. What did he do? Yep, on the coach, he got buzzing off his nut. Bear was in a different zone. BEAR puts his pen down in his pain. Looking out the lounge window, he sees that he has always been high looking at what he has put on the pad. Bear sits back in the chair slouching, his mind seeing his past and realising that he had always been under the influence of drink and drugs all his life as he lifts his eyes off the page. Bear sits up in his chair, stands up, walks over to the window, and stares at the clouds. My Ghost says to him, "Wow, we have lived a high life, literally.

"You know that you have to keep thinking of the times you were happy. The good thing is that you can now see where you went wrong, and now God is giving you a chance. You went to jail, whether you were guilty or not; you did your time. Unfortunately, you have lost your house, and you can't bring your dog back to life."

Bear's response to My Ghost was, "You are full of reminders, ain't you?"

"Well, I am you," replies My Ghost. Bear shrugs his shoulders and continues to look at the clouds. "Maybe I'll keep putting pen to paper, or later, I might do some drawings."

"THAT is a good idea to focus more on—" says My Ghost "—on your drawings. You have loads from jail, and now you can follow up on the awards. Keep the faith, because God helps those who help themselves."

Bear relaxes back on his daughter's settee and looks solemnly around. "My Ghost is right: if I have nothing, build from what I have," he says. Bear's mind wandered back to when he and the lady he was seeing then went to Brighton with his god sister Lol, and Lol looked down and saw the water between the joints of the timber. He recalls her panicking, and laughs at the memory. The look of fear on Lol's face was a picture as she screamed out, thinking she was going to fall between the joints.

After that episode, Bear recalls the three of them sitting and eating chips when a sea gull with a pair of balls tried to swoop in and take his chips. It was quite a picture to see him having a full-blown argument with a damn seagull. "Bless Lol, wish she was still here. God rest her soul."

Bear takes a deep breath as he recalls the episode, and his mind tries not to concentrate on the passing of his god sister; she was like a self-medicator; many a time she had stayed at Bear's in the past where he had to help her get straight. People have to realise that doing drink and drugs was easy but coming down was the hard part.

Bear's mind switches to a time he and a friend went into a café a few years ago where they adored two breakfasts. Well, Bear laughs at what happened. The lads were sitting at the table when the service came to the table. His mate was given a plate of food and Bear was given his breakfast in a bag. On remembering this, Bear could only laugh. If that wasn't a statement that blacks aren't allowed, then what is?

"You ok, Pops?" asks his daughter as she passes through the front room. "Yes, babe Bear, just think about it. You've got a lot to rebuild, you will be fine. Pops, just don't go backwards."

"I hear that," replies Bear, who then stands up and makes his way over to the window. As he looks out of the window, he does his usual stare straight into the clouds; that is his way of controlling himself. He lets his stresses float in the sky.

"I need to regroup." But in the past, Bear needed a problem to be able to operate, maybe because he was on the wrong path in the earlier years of his life and you always had to be ready for a change of direction or plan. What a mess being intoxicated and under the influence of drugs can do to your life and mind! Still, at least there was a light at the end of the tunnel. The question is, which tunnel do you take? Bear shakes his head as his mind comes back to Earth. He then recalls a few things he had written in prison and says, "Take some advice from what I have written; if prison was a walk in the park, then so should starting over again."

The doorbell rings; it's the postman. The envelope was too big to post through the letter box; it had the address of an art department; it kind of looked official on opening. Bear received three complimentary awards for his drawings called 'The Three Bears'. "Banes, look at this." He shows his daughter. "Look at your face."

She says, "I'm so proud of you." Bear sits rubbing his head. Anxiety steps in and makes him say, "Well, I got put away by people who didn't know me, and now I am getting awards from people who don't know me."

"Pops, you do know that all of us kids are proud of you, so keep your head up; life will work out for you. Remember, you always told us to let our stresses drift into the clouds, so keep level-headed like you say there is no right or wrong way to understand life; if there are billions of people, then there are billions of ways to live."

Bear takes in what pride his daughter was showing him, in his mind he knew that My Ghost was right in the advice or the way he shows Bear to understand the way he had lived in the past teaching Bear to see the fools he believed in and their expressions, their ways, the way he misunderstood. Bear saw that his life was not just about finding My Ghost his past of life mistakes or about him having to start rebuilding himself so late in life, he was being shown by My Ghost that nobody does become somebody. That is what the basics of Bear's life had been all about and it took a prison sentence to take notice and for Bear to see the realities of starting all over again and have the strength to see himself. "Raah!" Bear expresses, "I know I must get on with this change like there is no tomorrow."

"Wow," Bear looks around his surroundings, "life is nuts you never know what cards you are supposed to be dealt…" His pen found its way back into his hand. It rolled between his fingers as his mind was trying to understand all that was running through his soul. He smiles to himself, 'have I actually got my life back?' he writes and starts to describe a time in his life not too sure what he was writing, his pen does the usual writing making Bear overcome with realities from events the drink world and the drug world had let him expose himself to. Hours seem to pass as memory after memory – some good some bad flash onto the page. The pen was writing about mixed up vibes, why is it when you wanna think you seem not suffocate… The pen was rolling out word after word on the paper. His pen was doing most of his thinking for him.

Bear was truthfully on an emotional rollercoaster, which he didn't even realise until he heard My Ghost, "Look at what your pen is writing—seriously, look! I have been trying to make heads and tails of life; you found your calling; trust me, you have found your path through pen and paper; this time we have found the start of your new beginning. You know you can draw; you also know that when you draw, you get away from reality." My Ghost was trying to stop Bear from going back into the dark world of drugs.

"Do you not realise how much joy you brought to those jails and how much you got respected? Look at the literature you came out with, how many people came to you in Penn for advice, and also look at the art work and achievements you came out of jail with. Do not forget that people you did not know put you in jail, but people you did not know admire your hidden talents. STAY POSITIVE!"

Bear decides to go for a walk thinking about what was put into his mind by My Ghost. As he walks, he passes a few people who he can tell are high; he has the urge to ask them about it but changes his mind; it was his lust to get high that he had overcome; all it took was for him to think, *Raah, did I look like that when I used to buzz, or did I look worse?* He continues to walk into the small town, passing a few pubs and two or three hairdressers as he passes the nail salon. Bear looks up into the sky to see a bird of prey hovering above.

Looking at the everyday people going about their normal daily activities, Bear decides to sit outside the café, order a tea, and evaluate why he wants to get high just from seeing those people smash heads. My Ghost softly tells Bear not to think too hard about it because change always gives you as much self-doubt as self-belief, and that he must be the one to accept the way life is and not relish in the past. It has happened; good or bad, life has laid its path.

"Hello," a voice comes from an old lady asking, "Mind if I sit?" Bear nods his head and moves a chair out of the way. The old lady sits and smiles. "No worries," replies Bear, who then continues to ask the lady about the town he was in, as it had changed over the last 20 years.

"My dear, it has become a scary place; times have changed, and the younger people seem to have no morals, but it is like this everywhere I hear no manners or respect nowadays." The old lady had a sorry look on her face.

Bear intervenes, "But which is the right way to live? The way we were brought up in the olden days, life has moved forward so fast—look at the teenagers now."

The old lady smiles with her tired blue eyes; all of a sudden, they seem to sparkle. Then, out of the blue, the old lady says, "I know you; I'm sure you look so familiar to a lad I knew from Queen's Park. He used to drink in the Imperial before it was knocked." Bear had a shiver run through him as he realised she was talking about him; she even mentioned the car she had seen him drive.

Bear adjusts himself uncomfortably, waiting for a subject of badness, but that wasn't the memory he received from the lady. "It was you, wasn't it? My mind is not all there, but I'm sure you are who I am talking about; I'm sure you used to drink with a fellow called Barry or Bart." She stops and looks into Bear's eyes. "You know me, don't you?" Bear stares, and a name comes to mind— "is your name Yvonne or Evette?" The lady smiled, and her grey-blue eyes seemed to lift with warmth. The pair sit for over an hour talking and swapping stories about their lives. Bear ended up talking about his time in prison and the way his life had got worse to the point where it wasn't all bad.

"My, you have been through it, but from what you were saying about drink and drugs you must be proud of yourself."

"Thank you," Bear replies.

Yevette smiles and says sorry to be nosey, "But have I been too annoying?"

"No, it was a blessing for me," says Bear.

As Bear leaves the café, he says goodbye to Yevette and takes a slow walk back to his daughter's flat before he reaches, Bear sees an alley that leads to a field, so he decides to take a walk through the alley. As he is walking, he thinks in depth about how he is going to get his life together.

Bear comes to a bench in the alley underneath the street light. He thinks to himself, *I might go and see the Jazz* (one of his nephews that lived in the area). Jazz was deep like Bear and had serious respect for his uncle, which meant that Bear needed to chat with someone. Bear comes to a bench in the alley underneath the street light. He was going to have a conversation about My Ghost with Jazz, "He is one of the very few that would understand." Bear concludes to himself as he lights a fag and blows out the nicotine smoke into the street light, watching the smoke swirl and twist like it was alive.

Bear thinks about linking with Jazz, and then My Ghost says, "You do know that Jazz has a ghost—everyone has one." That being said loudly to Bear, and as he stares at the light in the alley, he jumps startled by the loudness of My Ghost in his head.

Bear sits thinking about everything right and says to himself, *I'm making my stress about my life changing harder than I thought.* He gets his phone and gives his nephew a bell. The phone rings, and Jazz answers the phone. "Yes, Uncs," he mentions how he heard about the house and what happened to his dog, which is what is unfortunately explained. "Bear in mind," in a serious voice, "that I will link up with you later today, yeah?"

Bear walks back up the alley to the main road without taking much notice; his body is feeling lost and his mind couldn't get its thought off of wanting to get high! Bear explained in a concerned tone as he walked down the road. Bear sits and wonders if My Ghost is real or if he is a figment of his imagination, but then My Ghost has to be real because My Ghost is Bear.

JAZZ'S bars

My Ghost reassures Bear that it was probably a blessing for him to talk with his nephew. Why, then, defeatist and thinking Bear, am I meeting up with my family because I'm lost and the only way up is to be what they believe with that thought in mind? Bear actually feels normal; he smiles at the thought that he was not a defeatist. He also realises he is all he has got, or so he thought. He gets a text message, and this is what was said:

When I hit rock bottom, I lay there awake,
Realising what was real and what was fake.
A new feeling of loneliness, regret and mistakes,
Putting trust in people who I thought were my mates.
The feeling of betrayal reaps through my veins.
Second guessing every path and decision I've made.
Putting all my energy to feed their own gain.
Every problem thrown at me I opened the gate,
To solve all their issues and their mental state.
Hide all my feelings that keep a smile on my face,
But I'm breaking down behind the bars in my brain.
Personally I don't know how much I can take
But giving up easily isn't one of my traits.
The willingness to succeed in this life I partake.
Keep positive daily when I don't feel great.
Prisoner of my own pride when it's easy to escape.
Bury my head into the sand if I was to break.
Narcotics to get by when I need to keep straight.
But my mind wanders uncomfortably when I'm up late.
Anxiety eating away at my pate.
No food to fuel me to get through the day.

Fatigued to the max I'm going insane.
My glass is half empty and I need to hydrate.
How do I break through my emotions that stand in my way?
To find logic and peace in my mind locked away.
I can't fail I'm a winner, TRUST me it's fate.
I will rise from my knees and move on from this place.

Rock Bottom

Bear looks at what he has been shown. My Ghost pipes up, "Do you really think that you are the only one trying to find a way forward? Look deeper Jazz has a ghost too, which he is showing you." Bear was kind of shocked, not at what he had seen but at the fact that life was naturally tripping him out. ROCK BOTTOM – that was a title for most people who have let life open their eyes.

Bear's mind concentrated on what he had just read; these were the words of his nephew's ghost. Bear was now understanding that he was not the only one going through loss in his life. "I care that he was also not alone when it came to light and that he needed help understanding the trauma."

His phone buzzes. Another message comes through. My Ghost whispers to him, "This is the power of change: you notice new ways and others notice you, and your message is worth read your message. Try to see the power that is being asked of you. See what is in front of you, Bear. Listen to the words of My Ghost."

He looks at the message it went like this:
I'm too strong to give up on what I want to achieve.
And let struggles in life shatter the things I believe.

I care a lot and wear my heart on my sleeve.
But it's hard to put aside feelings eating away at me.
The consequences that come with success aren't easy to see.
So the average person your bless with no pain to be eased
Which is typical for those with less stress and that are easily pleased!
While you are at rock bottom kicked down to your knees
'Everything has a cost nothing comes to you for free'
So be careful of those who show trails of greed.
Energy suckers who only come when they're in need.
But when you need help are nowhere to be seen
It's easy to get blinded don't by excitement I agree
But never forget who you are and the life you lead.
We don't give to receive but a little something back wouldn't go amiss every week
You're judged on every decision you make which makes it hard to speak
No one ever truly understands our grief.
Listen to reply with the wrong answers we need.
Ignoring our actual issues and pleas
So we turn to narcotics and drink to help us release
Built up tension that deprives us of sleep.
The inability to switch off and let our minds be free.
Causes the worst nightmares of the worst kind every time that we dream.
Sleepless nights might affect our ability to see how to get.
Constant pressure killing our self-beliefs.
And putting downers on jobs we have to complete.
Draining our energy trying to graft in this heat.
Climbing up mountains trying to find our peak.
Surviving by the skin of our teeth

Sometimes it feels like we're stuck on repeat
With no other option but defeat
But something hidden in me.
Tells me we're close to peace and not to give up on the life that we SEEK.

Bear shudders when he finishes reading. His mind is really tripping out; his motions are the same as his mind tripping. If you do not understand what Bear means, he means he is feeling venerable. His mind is trying to take in the meaning of what he has read. Obviously, because he was in a distant phase of his life, he knows he has to get to grips with his life. My Ghost was the clearest and best thing to happen to Bear since prison. Now she is free to do whatever she wants, but what is whatever?

"YOU GOT TO REGROUP." My Ghost had to intervene because he is Bear, so he knew Bear was on the verge of a relapse. "NO GETTING HIGH! NO GETTING DRUNK!" Bear stumbled as he heard those words— "you've got no faith, eh? Or is it that I have no faith in myself? My real sentence starts now, as I keep telling myself."

Bear stood still looking around the town he was in, staring at the locals and the traffic. "Do I go back to my daughters or do I look for someone to rent me a place?" All this was new to Bear, why? Because he had never had to rely on anyone before in his life and now was different.

Finding oneself after being drunk and high for so many years was a headache. But what did he do without thinking? He entered the nearest pub, not realising it was just a normal reaction when he was deep in thought. *YO,* he thinks, *ARE YOU FOR REAL LOOKING AROUND AND SEE WHERE*

YOU ARE, that was My Ghost waking Bear up to his movements. Bear freezes and looks around at the people getting on with their lives, thinking to himself, *Test myself first.*

Raaah! he thinks, his mind is in a mixed-up state, all types of thoughts are bombarding through his head, he shakes and adjusts the way he is standing, and life comes back into focus. "Wow," Bear says to himself, tripped out, "I got to get to grips with normality."

"DAMN RIGHT!" My Ghost says to him that there are a lot of people in touch with their ghosts.

"I understand that Bear responds, but everything about reality is hitting me. How can I get to grips with my life? I don't know where to start, and yet the things I have read have made my reality even harder knowing that there are people who are trapped in their thoughts just like me. Truthfully, I got to fix up and now."

Bear gets back into focus and starts to walk. As he turns the corner, he sees a young lass sitting outside the shop front; she has a quilt wrapped around her. He smiles and gives her some change and asks her if she is warm and would she like to have a cup of tea. They talk for a while as Bear listens to her tell of the bad things she had gone through and of the abuse she had been subjected to.

Bear feels distraught partly because he is now seeing that in the past when he was high and intoxicated, he had actually met a lady in a similar situation who he spent a lot of time talking to and associating with. So why was he distraught?

Why? Because he could not remember what happened to her, but in his heart, he knew that living on the street killed her. "THERE IS PAIN EVERYWHERE IN THIS WORLD!

thank you." My Ghost reminds him that we have been so high that we took life for granted. "Come on, say goodbye to this lass, and get back to your daughter's; don't forget you are on probation." Bear says goodbye to the lass, promising to pass back later and get her something home. With a smile she says goodbye and thankyou. Bear leaves her his cigarettes and heads back to his daughter's.

As he walks into the lounge, he sees a pen. He gets his pad out and starts to write; his pen was on form, I tell ya.

It starts to put words on the paper, and in the background, there is some old school reggae playing. Bear is now more relaxed as his pen writes fluently and quite quickly.

My days have been weird and mixed up. I need to get this stress out of me. I am lost but not weak. I know that a new beginning is what I must seek. I need to adjust in this outside world. That little stint I had in prison gave me rest and cleaned me up, but I feel a relapse coming, and the worst of it is I think I need to just survive.

Self-doubt

Bear had grown up with the abnormal ways of the streets, so messed up sights weren't really upsetting, but now that he was actually seeing life through straight eyes, his concept had changed; he hadn't realised that there was such a difference in people's attitudes. He now understood that the reason he was subjected to the world of drink and drugs was not for the sorrows, but because it was how he fit in, and that he was also left alone by the normal judgements.

Bear had been blessed with many offspring fair play he didn't have the 2.4 kids but he knew they were his strength and he had done well to keep his flock close by being truthful and not hiding when he was high (nothing to be proud of but he was in a world that if it affected his kids he could deal with helping them also being in the street world his kids had a lot of characters protecting them and people of all sorts looking out for them).

By putting his pen to the pad, Bear took his uneasiness away; it was a total release for him. Well, well it must have been what carried him through jail. He had no regrets about his sentence; his only regret was that he got jailed because of the world he was in. My Ghost feels Bear's vibes and says, "They are saying you have really got to get off that trail of thought. There is a new life you are going through. There is nothing wrong with carrying memories, but you must respect and learn from your losses. You must let yourself get back up, but with happier thoughts."

There are many people with their ghosts coming to light, and it is up to you to help them see their ghosts. Only then can changes happen in life, and many of us have a lack of understanding.

Learn from past experiences and be able to see the truth in your ways. Bear put his pen down, and his mind drifts in thought as he remembers situations and attitudes he has experienced. Staring out of the lounge window, he notices something going on.

His pen writes down as he watches out of the window. *Is that what I was like on the street in public eyes? Scoring drugs thinking that I wasn't being seen, how dumb could I have been?* As Bear thought about the movements, he noticed how the dealer was aggressive in his motions and how sheepish the buyers were, nuts really, but when you are in that world, life is oblivious to you.

Only now Bear was seeing life from an outside point of view. He rubs his head in despair, realising that if he hadn't gone through jail and also the process that he is going through, his pen was now writing what he was seeing, but at the same time Bear could now have an opinion about himself without a let-down aura or self-pity but with actual self-control. The more he noticed the outside world, the more his body was slowly sinking into the wrong way of thinking, or some would say into a Relapse.

My Ghost did not have an answer for the reunion, but he knew that Bear had to go through these misconclusions about himself. Bear stops writing and rereads what had been put on the pages again. He stares out of the lounge window, watching each way these addicts and dealers walked. He observes every movement that is made. He puts his pen down, taking notice of his opinions that he had formed after looking at what was going on. "Raaah" was all that Bear could let come out of his mouth.

He could feel a taste that he hadn't felt for some time, the taste of high, a buzz, or whatever you want to call it within himself, he knew he would be having a taste. Bear stops staring out of the window. His heart felt so low that life was giving him another slap, a reality check. How many of them had he experienced in his life?

Again, he stares out the window; this time he is staring at the clouds as if to find an answer. To explain how he was feeling, his mind floated into the sky, trying to let his cluck release from his body, knowing it was not right for him to want or miss his old habits. Within 5–10 minutes he is back in control of himself, reluctantly, he is back in the real world of his. Bear sits pondering his life, truly understanding that he had never been like this before.

Funny how life experiences can change a person's chain of thoughts; surely it must be age that helps you with the answers. Bear silently hopes that My Ghost would intervene and put some sense in his mind, but no, My Ghost stays silent. *Why?* thought Bear to himself, still looking out of the window.

As time passed, Bear starts to get back to himself. He shrugs his shoulders, picks up his pen, and starts to flow words onto his pad.

"Where do I start now? I'm out. I must get to grips with these feelings and I must start these changes, or rather, change for this new start. I have to face as usual." He tries to get the answer but is now understanding that he is the change he was looking for; he now has to believe in himself for the first time. Had he more skeletons to let go of, or was he really in the world of failures? "HEY! Stop!" My Ghost makes an appearance. "How are you not in control? Why are you questioning yourself over and over again? Have you learned nothing?"

WHY HAVE A NEGATIVE VIEW? BECAUSE TWO NEGATIVES WILL NOT MAKE A POSITIVE. My Ghost points out just some food for thought; he says, "Bear, understand, life has a time and place for each and every scenario."

He then returns to his actions, thinking to himself that maybe next time I'm with my probation officer, I will bring up my thoughts. He thinks to himself, *I need to get out of here and be on the road where I can be me.* Bear concludes that he had a life before jail that may not have been the best, but he was off his nut and now he is in a reality check. If there is such a thing as normalcy.

TRUTHFULLY

My Ghost is probably the best mental experience Bear has had the pleasure to get to know. Why? Because he found himself a changed person in thought and deed. The phrasing and meaning of these in-depth conversations has taught Bear that in life, before you can see anything, you must see yourself.

AND THERE IS MORE TO BE TOLD.

FROM ME MY GHOST remember

Everything is a balanced mess to be spread evenly

Everything in life is a test of your patience and

How you handle situations,

Learn from your mistakes.

Gain qualifications, in life.

Also refrain from unnecessary complications.

LIFE is very simple.

YOU will see that sometimes you can cause distress,

Just be truthful enjoy the power of owning up to you faults.

It is true when it rains it pours.

Courtesy is not to be ignored.

Fuelled by hurt and blindness.

Can make your future hazy.

That means you have run your course so
TAKE A BREAK YOUR EYES ARE OPEN
YOU NOW ARE TO HAVE CHOICES
BLESS
MY GHOST

Jazz was Bear's nephew, and he had sent Bear a text message showing his ghost in rap form. "Funny how people get affected by life, isn't it?" My Ghost intervenes. "You do know that before you can advise anyone, you have to be able to show some form of proof or belief before you get taken seriously."

Bear says to My Ghost, "I've been waiting for your intake for a few weeks now, but no, you blank me now. I don't know what to say obviously, with not long being out of jail and having to start all over again, I just do not want to go through all that all over again. I am too old for this, and I would not wish to go try and fail this for events, which in turn of events is hard to take in as I was a mash head, it would be too easy to give up." Bear is starting to get stressed out. Why? Because reality is here, and also because if not for those turns of events, Bear knew there would not be My Ghost, there would not have been the experience, he frowns at his thoughts of the last few years and stares into the sky as he always does when he is stressed.

Then Jazz's bars (lyrics) come into his mind, which seem to mellow his aura. *Sort out the way*, Bear thinks. It makes Bear calm to actually see his nephew's ghost. Bear could now see that the way he had put pen to paper was the reason for his change of ways. He could now believe in the way he was seeing life for himself.

Bear bowls down the road off to see his probation officer, which really is a waste of time, and he has no help whatsoever from them in getting sorted out. Once they bother Bear, he surmises to offer him shared accommodation; Hell no! is his answer.

"You know you have another year and a half left," My Ghost whispers, "and furthermore, where are you going now, uh?" Bear doesn't know where he is now going. "That is no good for you to be so ignorant; you're only being ignorant to yourself, and that is not good, is it really? Think about times in the past when you felt like this and what happened; relapses have a pattern, and you should be aware of it." My Ghost is gone. At the same time that Bear is dealing with his episodes, feeling lost, but he knows that he cannot complain because, on the other side of the world, he knows that there are people in worse predicaments than him in reality, so he is still better off than these unfortunate people. So, Bear's message for himself was to try and be better himself so he could in some way teach or help to improve other's lives. He smiles at his thoughts.

Jazz's lyrics are now loud in Bear's mind, and the words he has written about My Ghost echo in his brain. Most days, Bear mumbles, "I need to go and plot up somewhere. Why am I doing this crap to myself? If any of my children came to me with the same situation as what I have, what advice would I give them?"

That was the most sensible advice Bear had given himself for a long time. He stopped in his tracks. In his imagination, he saw one of his sons asking him for advice. Bear must take it all in; his mind was on a mission. Bear couldn't wait to get himself into a more secure way of living; all he wanted to do was meet other ghosts so he could help people. "I wonder what is in store for me now."

Bear goes back to his cousin's house and says hello to everyone who is in the kitchen. "Yo! You good?" Bear nods and replies, "I'm always good," and walks up the stairs to his room. On entering, he looks across to the window. The view is so breathtaking that Bear actually finds himself walking around the bed and getting his pencils out.

Bear does his usual when he is feeling low: he stares out of the window, his eyes fixed on one cloud that resembles a mountain scenery. Seeing as My Ghost hasn't really been around properly for a few weeks, Bear has a few things in his head he needed to deal with, obviously a new chapter to deal with, so he starts to make a mental note in his mind. "Seeing as My Ghost has been a bit vacant, I still have to face the realities that I am going through."

His past flies through his mind, a bit ridiculously, he says to himself. He is now deciding how to be totally honest with himself.

Bear saw that he had no regrets; he had learned from the way life is that you see a lot when you are on a different path: him going to prison, My Ghost, him being homeless—in a way, it was a blessing in disguise. He must move on, but why? At the end of the day, he has always been his own person, regardless of whether he was drunk or on drugs. All of a sudden, My Ghost intervenes, "And the first thing you have to do is have some time to yourself.

"All the time you stress about what cards life has dealt you, you will not see clearly, embrace the new start, embrace the new change, and embrace the fact that a new story has begun. Let us see what chapters unfold with those last words." My Ghost is gone.

There is more to come – hardship, pain, suffering, and love are what a person MUST GO THROUGH IN ORDER TO BE REAL, FEEL, AND EMBRACE LIFE.